Why We Feel "Road Rage"

... And Why It's Your Fault!

Exposing the Culprits Who Frustrate Good Drivers

Words and
Illustrations by
David Allan

FNA Publishers
Webster, MA

Library of Congress Control Number: 2008939295

Published by
FNA Publishers, LLC
P.O. Box 214
Webster, MA 01570

ISBN: 978-0-9822008-0-3

Printed in the United States of America

Interior illustrations by David Allan
Cover illustration by David Allan and Pete Stoppel (www.solosplace.com)
Design by Carol Daly and Cecile Kaufman

Dedication

To my wife, Amy, who never stops smiling . . . even when riding in a car with me.

And to Mike Coogan, the most selfless man I know.
(Branding & Marketing $\longrightarrow$ cooganmf@yahoo.com)

Acknowledgments

First of all, I would like to thank the good people at Google for providing affordable "Sketchup" software to the masses . . . it's an incredibly intuitive, well-designed 3D application (www.sketchup.com).

And my thanks to FormFonts® (www.formfonts.com), whose models were instrumental in creating most of this book's illustrations.

CONTENTS

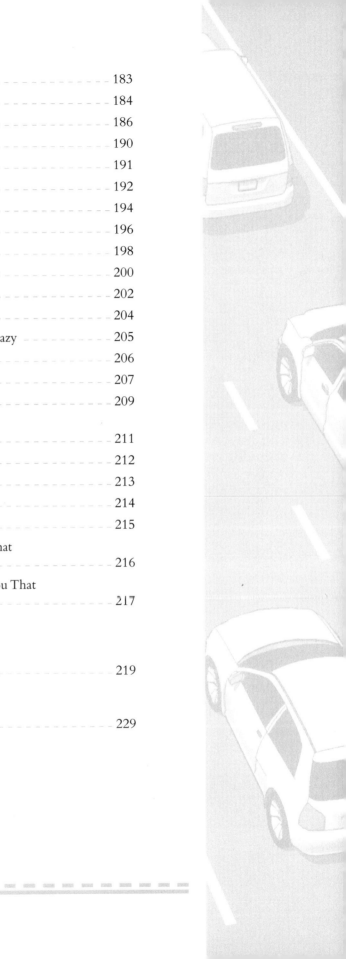

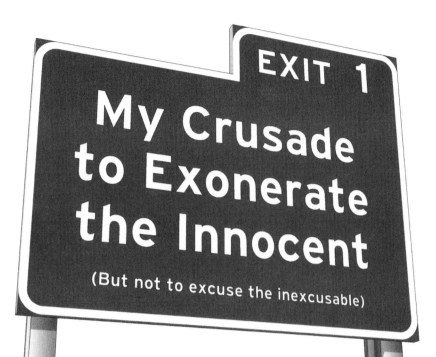

My Crusade to Exonerate the Innocent

(But not to excuse the inexcusable)

A re you a good person whose patience is often tested when you get behind the wheel? When you become frustrated by bad drivers, do your passengers ever act as if somehow *you're* to blame? Do you find yourself defending your emotions while the true culprits behind them are completely ignored? If you answered yes to any of these questions, then fasten your seatbelt because I'm about to take you on a joyride!

Many books have been written about road rage, traffic, and other related topics. Most have purported to reveal the *supposed* root causes of aggressive driving, advising us on how to control our emotions and avoid provoking others. Well *this* isn't one of those books! Instead, it's a concise, illustrated, humorous read for people like you and me who refuse to waste time on psychobabble. Road rage is a very simple issue, and this book is the first of its kind to cut through the nonsense and explain it as such.

Contrary to what the media would like you to believe, reportable incidents of road rage *behavior* are extremely rare. The true epidemic is the millions of good people out there who struggle to control their emotions when provoked by careless, inconsiderate, and annoying drivers.

This book, my friends, is for *you*!

 In the Beginning . . .

As far back as I can recall, I've been aggravated by inconsiderate, annoying, and just plain stupid people.

For example, I can remember my first drawer ding like it was yesterday.

And I'll never forget the first time I was stuck behind a left-lane hog.

Yes . . . this book has been a very, very long time in the making.

Pass/Fail Grading of the Human Race

I was introduced to pass/fail grading in the second grade. Our teacher tried to explain that normal grading was sometimes thought to promote "undesirable competition among students." Huh? Even at eight years old I recognized nonsense when I heard it. This new grading system would do nothing but *discourage* excellence. When I studied hard enough to deserve an A, I would receive the same passing grade as someone who barely scraped by with a D. Oh, that just wasn't right.

But I've developed an exaggerated form of pass/fail grading that has one perfect application: the human race. As a result, each book in my Why It's Your Fault™ series is based upon the premise that there are two distinct classes of people in the world: those who *feel* frustration (Class A) and those who *cause* it (Class F).

 Those of us in Class A "get it." We're thoughtful and considerate. We're achievers. We hunger for knowledge, and we constantly strive to improve ourselves and the world around us. And when it comes to the road, we're coordinated, intelligent, and careful drivers.

 On the other hand, people in Class F (let's call them "F"s, shall we?) are inherently thoughtless and inconsiderate—traits that lead to a complete disregard for the welfare of others. "F"s cause endless frustration in others by way of their offensive behavior.

For example, "F"s are those jerks who dart across traffic to avoid missing their exit, who never turn off their high beams, who don't turn right on red when they're supposed to, who slow down when they see a speed trap, even when they're not speeding . . . even when the speed trap is on the *other* side of the highway.

"F"s take up two parking spaces. They stop at the first open gas pump instead of the last, making you drive around them. They rarely use turn signals, and yet when they do they fail to turn them off. When you attempt to pass them on a two-lane road, they accelerate. When turning left, they don't leave room for you to go past them on the right. The infamous population of Class F also includes rubber-neckers, litterbugs, and drunk drivers.

And by the way, "F"s are as inane and confoundingly irritating *off* the road as they are on it. They exist in the form of vehicle salespeople who never shut up, office workers who surf the Internet all day, people who don't say "thank you" when doors are held open for them, movie patrons who eat popcorn with their mouths open, twits who talk loudly on cell phones in public places . . . the list, unfortunately, is endless.

Do the people of Class A become frustrated? Yes, we do. Is it our fault? No, it is not. "F"s are to blame!

⟨⟩ Stop Poking Me!

As a teen I discovered that frustration is neither a sudden nor a self-generated emotion. Instead, it builds over time and is directly triggered by the actions of others. Look up the word "frustrate" in a dictionary and you'll find it typically defined as an "action verb *with* object":

> To *make* (plans, efforts, etc.) worthless or of no avail;

> To *prevent* from accomplishing a purpose or fulfilling a desire;

> To *induce* feelings of frustration in (a person).

Since road rage is clearly a form of frustration, I contend that it is predominantly caused by the repetitive, offensive actions of "F"s. Our road rage emotions—our feelings of frustration—are their fault. Period.

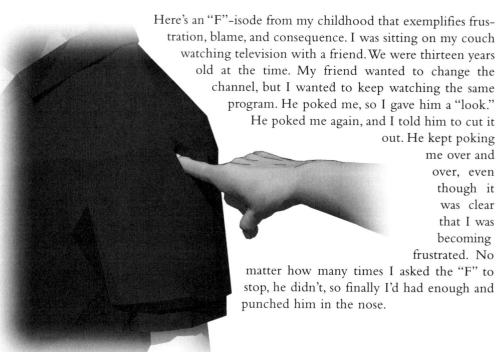

Here's an "F"-isode from my childhood that exemplifies frustration, blame, and consequence. I was sitting on my couch watching television with a friend. We were thirteen years old at the time. My friend wanted to change the channel, but I wanted to keep watching the same program. He poked me, so I gave him a "look." He poked me again, and I told him to cut it out. He kept poking me over and over, even though it was clear that I was becoming frustrated. No matter how many times I asked the "F" to stop, he didn't, so finally I'd had enough and punched him in the nose.

He ran screaming out of the house, running right past my father (of *course*) who was in the kitchen. My father stormed into the living room and demanded that I explain myself. I blurted out every kid's favorite excuse—"*He* started it!"—at which point I was sent to my room for the rest of the night . . . no dinner . . . no television. What kind of twisted lesson was that? At the time I thought my dad should have been proud of me for throwing such a solid and well-deserved punch.

Well, we're all adults now, so we don't have the latitude of punching "F"s in the nose when they frustrate us. But once in a while, we certainly feel justified in poking them back. When we do this on the road, say by speeding around an annoying "F" once we have the chance, we're often spotted by a police officer and cited for reckless driving. "But, officer, you didn't see what led up to my frustration . . . he started it!" "Yes, how interesting . . . here's your ticket." It's a bit like being unfairly sent to your room by your father, don't you think?

As you read this book, it will become readily apparent to you that I really, *really* despise "F"s. For me, writing this book was therapeutic . . . the next best thing to punching them in the nose. Hopefully you'll find it great therapy as well.

Measuring the Problem

Please note that Class F consists of the following three categories:

> Morons—"F"s who are too clueless to understand the difference between right and wrong.

> Twits—inconsiderate "F"s who understand the difference but don't care.

> Jerks—those who intentionally aggravate others.

To effectively measure these characteristics, I developed the "F" Meter in partnership with the renowned research firm of Mee, Miselph, and Iye. The meter shown here will appear throughout the book to indicate each "F"-isode's severity. You'll learn that hapless morons generate relatively low readings, inconsiderate twits are usually more frustrating, and annoying jerks always generate the highest "F" Meter readings.

Crime and Punishment

I must admit that I often fantasize about "F"s being spectacularly punished for their bad behavior, but like every member of Class A, I've accepted that it's wrong to take matters into my own hands.

So instead I imagine a world where actions have consequences . . . where there's a great defender . . . a guardian . . . a hero to the "A"s.

When provoked, I conjure up images of an **"F"-INATOR** emerging from out of nowhere to inflict judgment and retribution on behalf of "A"s everywhere. This gigantic vehicle would come equipped with a Swiss Army knife of "power tools," any one of which could be used to instantly punish "F"s in ways that those of us in Class A can only dream about. The **"F"-INATOR** is the world's first Fault Utility Vehicle, or "FUV."

And how would the **"F"-INATOR** know when its services were needed?

We'd imagine an "F" Signal, of course!

Ignorance Is Bliss

While the **"F"-INATOR** provides comforting fantasies, we also need to effectively cope with morons, twits, and jerks in the real world. The best approach I've found for blissfully dealing with "F"s is to just ignore them. "F"s are weak-minded, needy people, and therefore I suggest that you refuse to give them the attention they crave.

In those rare cases when you're actually confronted by "F"s, make it abundantly clear that they're insignificant specks in your universe. Shun them and virtually refuse to acknowledge their existence. This approach drives them absolutely crazy, and it usually doesn't inflame matters into anything more than an exchange of words. The "F"-isode later in this book entitled "Wrong Turn on Red" provides a classic example.

To my new recruits into "Allan's Army," I say do not, for any reason, allow "F"s to stir your emotions beyond the point of self-control. When you lose control, you actually become one of them. Sorry.

And don't even give them the satisfaction of flipping them off . . . that's beneath us. If you can't resist the urge to express your displeasure with "sign language," just turn your hand toward the sky and share the universal "What-an-F" sign. But even that small gesture can trigger temper in some "F"s, so use discretion.

Finally, it's time we improved our language, even inside our own vehicles. Profanity tends to create more stress than it relieves (especially in passengers), and "F"s simply aren't worth it. This book is about replacing anger with laughter, derision, and ridicule. Foul language usually doesn't fit the bill.

Note: You can find new curse jargon on our website (www.roadragebook.com), which is updated regularly with user input.

⬦ The Cast of Characters

Class A

"A"s in this book will be driving bright, snappy vehicles that reflect their owners' inherent outlook on life.

Class F

"F"s will be seen driving dull, grey vehicles that match their dull, feeble minds.

(For example, when we asked a group of "F"s to arrange themselves in an orderly manner for the photo shoot, this is what they came up with.)

. . . and starring:

Your intrepid champion of the open road . . .

ME!

When It's Right to Be Politically Correct

Let it be known that this book does not, in *any* way, target the mentally handi-capped. My definition of a moron, for example, is a person who possesses a fully functional brain but is too lazy to use it.

 And when you see special plates for the physically handicapped, ex-POWs, veterans, etc., please cut them some slack. You don't know what they've had to go through or are going through now. This book supports their right to special treatment.

Old people are also off-limits. They should obviously hand over their keys at some point, but just try to imagine having to do that yourself . . . we'll all be in their shoes one day. Elderly folks whose spouses have died or whose children live out of state still need to run errands from time to time. They deserve understanding and patience far beyond what we'd offer most others. So no "F" talk when it comes to the elderly.

IS ANYONE DRIVING THIS CAR ??

Enjoyment vs. Education

For those of you in Class A, this book should be a pleasure read. You should enjoy it if for no other reason than to know there are others out there who share your pain. Depending upon your mood, you might even laugh a little.

"F"s, on the other hand, should consider this a remedial textbook. In that vein, I'll commit right here and now to giving a significant discount to any driver's educa-tion instructor who agrees to use my book as a teaching aid in the hope that it will prevent as many new drivers as possible from becoming future "F"s.

Why You Should Listen to Me

You may ask what qualifications I possess to warrant your taking my advice.

First of all, like most members of Class A, I was born with an inn-"A"-te driving sensibility. I'm always attentive, I'm always careful, I'm always efficient, and I'm always considerate (all right . . . I'll admit that with "F"s I'm not *always* considerate). I've never been in an accident with another vehicle and I never will be . . . unless some "F" out there does something so stupid that the laws of physics literally prevent its avoidance.

Second, as expressed earlier, I've been studying and cataloging the habits of "F"s for decades, so I know an "F" when I see one.

Third, I pay attention to every little detail about everything . . . especially about people . . . *especially* about "F"s. In other words, I'm as anal-retentive as they come. If there was an anal-retentive contest, I'd win hands down. (Just imagine what the trophy would look like!)

And lastly I'm a time freak . . . there's too little of it. No, Mr. Jagger, time is *not* on my side. When my wife reminds me to "live for the moment," I tell her that I do live for the moment . . . just not *this* one.

Well, enough about me . . . let's hit the road, shall we?

EXIT 2

The Need to Impede

Slowing the progress of other drivers brings "F"s a twisted sense of satisfaction. I call this affliction "the need to impede." "F"s often put this under the guise of exercising their patience. My response? They should save their exercising for the gym.

This "EXIT" covers such benign blunders as "F"s who can't understand simple traffic signs, confusion over the proper use of cruise control, and traffic jams created by "F"s loitering in the left lane. Dangerously dumb moves include reading while driving, cutting off other drivers, and speeding in the snow.

What's My Sign?

Let's start with the irrefutable fact that people who drive below posted speeds are "F"s. They do this either because they have nowhere to go or because they're satisfying their need to impede. So to help them find their way—and to keep them out of *our* way—I propose that all public roads be retrofitted with the improved speed signs shown below.

The first thing you'll notice is that speed limit signs will now become speed *minimum* signs. Those of us in Class A have always intuitively understood this.

For you "F"s out there, these signs will now state the obvious: that you should generally travel at *least* as fast as posted speeds . . . 45 mph in the first example.

And please notice that highway speed signs will now indicate different speeds for different lanes. This is a foreign concept to many of you, but it just might urge you toward participating in a little ritual we "A"s like to call "passing."

OLD

SPEED LIMIT 45

SPEED LIMIT 55

SPEED LIMIT 65

NEW

SPEED MINIMUM 45

SPEED MINIMUM 65 | 55

SPEED MINIMUM 75 | 70 | 65

"F"s, are you still with me? ('Cause I can write a little slower if you need me to . . .)

One more thing—be advised that a lobbying effort is under way to pass legislation which would allow police officers to force you from the highway if you travel below the speed minimum without good reason. In the interim, for those of you who are too clueless to periodically check your speedometer, here's a handy tip:

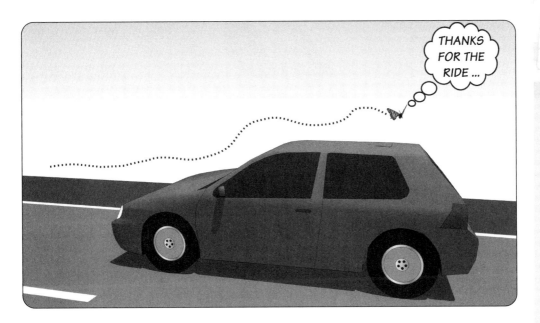

If a bug has time to dodge out of the way before it splats onto your windshield, then you might want to pick up the pace a bit.

⬦⊢ Please Explain Your Obsession with the Left Lane

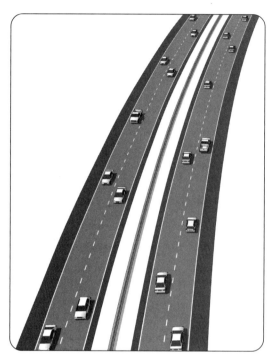

The scene to the left displays what a multilane highway is supposed to look like. Slower vehicles are traveling in the right lane, and faster vehicles are in the left lane.

Congestion is light.

Everyone is happy.

But look what happens when "F"s join the party. They become obsessed with the left lane, showing no consideration whatsoever for anyone but themselves. And once they take over that lane, they add insult to injury by matching the speed of vehicles in the right lane(s). Traffic becomes heavily congested as "F"s essentially turn multilane highways into single-lane roads.

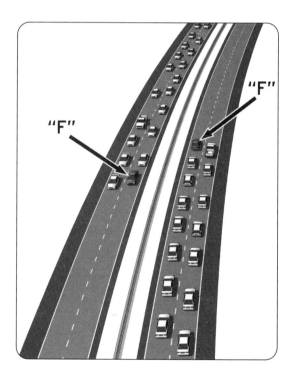

"F"

"F"

You'll be pleased to learn that some states are *finally* passing laws to penalize these left-lane slowpokes.

Wouldn't it be nice if those laws applied everywhere?

By the way, I've come up with a solution to this problem: revolutionary "A"-daptive cruise control outfitted to every vehicle. This new technology would allow a *trailing* vehicle to "push" a leading vehicle when it was traveling too slowly. As opposed to giving "F"s the finger, we could now give them the whole hand.

You may view this as pure science fiction, but you'll soon see that in some situations this technology is fully functional right now.

It's a Car, Not a Phone Booth

An "F" attempting to drive while talking on a cell phone is quite possibly the most common source of road rage emotions.

Those of us in Class A are capable of doing both things at once because our brains can simultaneously process multiple inputs. And most importantly, when push comes to shove, we will *always* give the road precedence over our phone call.

But "F"s can't walk and chew gum at the same time. When engaged in a cell phone conversation, their driving becomes frighteningly erratic. Their limited gray matter places emphasis on the phone call and, once that occurs, their focus shifts almost entirely away from the road, causing random speed changes and unpredictable swerving.

Their behavior would indicate that they sometimes forget altogether that they're *still driving a vehicle*! When the son of a friend of mine sees outlandish driving like this, he says, "They must be either drunk or on a cell phone." Let's hope we never cross paths with an "F" who's drunk *and* on a cell phone.

The latest trend, which is far more flagrant than the last, is *texting* while driving. Are they kidding?! Why don't they take a nap in the back seat while they're at it?

An "F" talking on a cell phone or texting while driving makes about as much sense as a doctor doing so during a critical surgery: none.

Hold on a minute . . . do I hear a phone ringing?

 **Speed Demon**

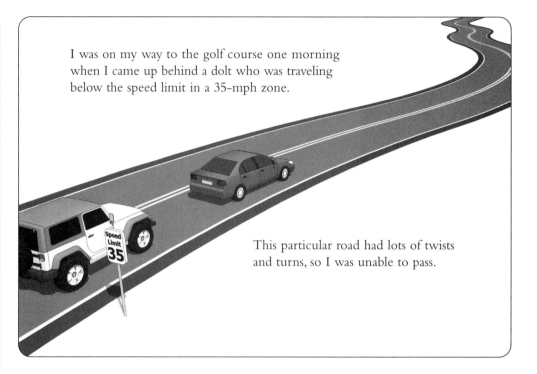

I was on my way to the golf course one morning when I came up behind a dolt who was traveling below the speed limit in a 35-mph zone.

This particular road had lots of twists and turns, so I was unable to pass.

Once we reached a passing zone, however, I took off and began to overtake him.

Unbelievably, the "F" accelerated to prevent my maneuver!

I hit almost 60 mph before getting past the "demon," unable to move back into the right lane until *after* the passing zone had ended.

I damn near hit a pickup truck head on!

At that point, I tapped on my brakes to express my "displeasure," which inadvertently caused the "F" to lock up *his* brakes. When I saw this, an appealing vision suddenly popped into my head.

But then I thought better of my actions—I realized that it just wasn't right to put another life at risk.

After all, what did that poor tree ever do to me?

ⓨ Mirror, Mirror in the Car . . . Who's the Biggest "F" by Far?

This "F"-isode shows me following yet another "F" who's been driving slowly in the left lane. Since passing on the right is generally less safe, I give him a moment to move over. His constant glances in the rearview mirror betray his intentions—he sees me there and realizes I'm in a hurry—so he now does one of the following two things:

(1) He creeps over into the middle lane as slowly as possible in a lame attempt to teach me some sort of lesson.

(2) He waits for me to become perturbed and pull around him on the right, and once I do that he swerves into my lane to cut me off.

I swear—the following message should be stamped onto the mirrors of every "F"-mobile:

> OBJECTS IN MIRROR ARE MORE
> PISSED OFF THAN THEY APPEAR!

The Moron Roller Coaster

I suspect that many of you have witnessed a moron roller coaster at one time or another, which occurs when an "F" tries to emulate cruise control by keeping his accelerator pedal in exactly the same position. This, of course, results in his speed fluctuating wildly when changing elevation.

There's a section of my daily commute where a six-lane divided highway goes over a series of hills in a relatively short distance. Leading into this area is a long down-hill stretch. One night on my way home, traffic was light so I was in the middle lane. Coming down that long hill in the left lane was a car outpacing mine. I incorrectly assumed it was driven by a Class-A friend.

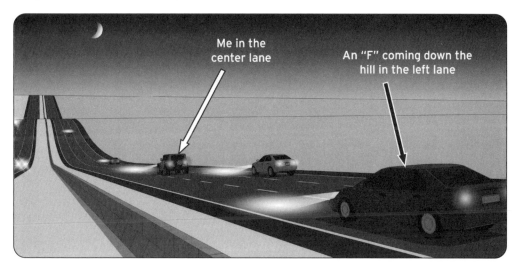

Me in the center lane

An "F" coming down the hill in the left lane

The car passed me as we came into the first valley and then pulled back into the middle lane in front of me. So far so good.

But as we started uphill, his steady-pedal approach caused him to decelerate. Since my cruise control was engaged and fully functional, I was forced to pull into the left lane to pass *him*. It was now clear that I was dealing with a mindless "F".

When we crested the next mound, he pulled out to the left again and began passing me down the next hill . . . but this time he didn't make it far enough past me to pull back into the middle lane.

And now for the crescendo of this imbecilic "amusement" park ride: up the next incline, I out-accelerated the "F" a second time (thanks again to the aforementioned cruise control).

As a result, he pulled back into the middle lane behind me and flashed his high beams.

At this point I couldn't decide whether to laugh or cry. This "F" actually thought *I* was the one changing speeds, so he decided to punish me with his high beams.

It reminded me of the movie, *The Sixth Sense*, in which certain dead people didn't realize they were dead. This "F" was oblivious to the fact that he too was dead in his own right . . . brain-dead, that is.

⬦ The Big Pedal on the Right

After I had followed an "F" at about 60 mph in the left lane for what seemed like an eternity, he finally made his way clear of vehicles in the middle lane. Of course, he didn't move over at that point.

Therefore, once I could do it safely, I pulled into the middle lane and came back up to an acceptable speed.

SIMPLETON.

Then something remarkable happened—the "F" suddenly discovered the purpose behind that big pedal on the right, so instead of him impeding me at 60 mph in the left lane, we were now both going 80 mph.

It was like dealing with a five-year-old. After being "in charge" there for a while, he couldn't bear the thought of losing his place at the head of the line.

For my colleagues in Class A: the next time you pull up behind one of these left-lane intellectual delinquents, try this little test (but only when there's no traffic). If you want to make him go faster, pull into the lane to his right. I guarantee you he will accelerate. Pull back in behind him and he'll decelerate. Repeat this pattern until boredom sets in.

A final warning to the "F"s: obey the improved speed *minimum* signs, engage your cruise control, and stay in the appropriate lane.

Either that or deal with my new friend . . .

It's a Car, Not a Diner . . . or a Library . . . or a . . .

Hey, "F"s . . . getting food "to go" doesn't automatically mean "to drive." If you can eat or drink using one free hand *without* taking your eyes off the road, then be my guest. But that doesn't mean you're allowed to awkwardly steer with your knees while devouring an oversize-me-super-steak-and-cheese-sub-with-the-works! The rule is this: at least one hand on the wheel and both eyes on the road at all times . . . no exceptions.

Here's another one that really annoys me: those of you who read while driving.

> Sometimes it's a map (*go buy a nav system, you misguided oaf!*).
> Other times it's a book (*um, ever heard of books on tape?*).
> I once even saw one of you "F"s working on a laptop computer while sipping a latte (*hey! wake up and smell the coffee before I "grind" you to a halt*).

Oh, how it drives me to distraction when I see you driving while distracted!

In fact, I fully suspect that some of you are reading this very book right now while driving. Well . . . inasmuch as I appreciate how difficult it must be for you to stop reading my masterpiece now that you've started it, please put it down before you hurt someone, okay?

Make Up Your Mind, Not Your Face

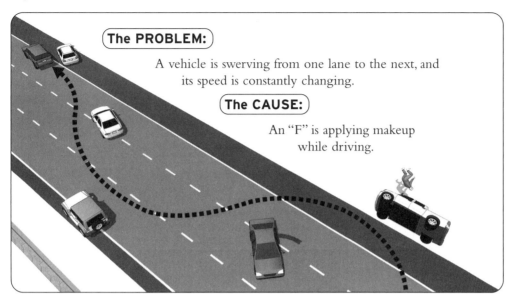

The PROBLEM:

A vehicle is swerving from one lane to the next, and its speed is constantly changing.

The CAUSE:

An "F" is applying makeup while driving.

Here are a few reasons an "F" will cite for pulling this move:

> "I lost track of time" (*then take a course in time management*).

> "I could lose my job if I'm late" (*not if you're a hard worker, you won't*).

> "I had to get the kids ready for school" (*the fact that you have kids at all is proof that natural selection doesn't always work*).

This ranks high on the list of road rage stunts because, like texting and reading, applying makeup also takes visual focus away from the road. I've actually seen this done by a woman with a baby in the back seat (in broad daylight)! But this isn't strictly a female phenomenon—I've also observed men driving while shaving or combing their hair. What a joke.

"F"s attending to personal grooming while driving gives a whole new meaning to the concept of vanity plates. In fact, here's an idea: let's pass a law *requiring* "F"s to use vanity plates.

To alert the rest of us that an "F" was in our midst, each plate would be marked with a huge red "No F" symbol . . . a modern-day scarlet letter, as it were. Wouldn't that be nice?

⑤ The Blind Leading the Blind

"A"s will only pass on the right if there's an "F" impeding the left lane. Conversely, "F"s pass on the right solely out of ignorance, very often hovering in another driver's blind spot while they're at it.

Those of us in Class A are attentive and therefore will never inadvertently pull into the right lane, even with an "F" in our blind spot. We accomplish this by utilizing the swiveling characteristic of our heads, which are mounted on these things called necks. That and our mirrors.

An "F" begins to pass on the right but then hovers in my blind spot.

But if I've seen this next example once I've seen it a hundred times:

"F"#1 hovers in the blind spot of "F"#2 . . .

. . . "F"#2 is clueless, so he doesn't realize #1 is there . . .

. . . and therefore #2 drifts into the right lane and cuts off #1.

At this point, I can't help but laugh out loud as *both* morons are shocked by this action. "F"#1 can't possibly understand why "F"#2 would cut him off. Frequently #1 will use his horn or high beams to express his frustration, all the while being responsible for the problem in the first place. At the same time, "F"#2's lack of attention causes him to wonder where the heck #1 came from.

Here's another near-collision I witnessed during the course of writing this book. As depicted in the first frame below, "F"#1 was passing in the left lane (for once), and "F"#2 was coming up behind a slow-moving truck in the right lane.

In the second frame, you'll see that "F"#1 carelessly pulled into the middle lane without considering that "F"#2 had to do the same thing in order to pass the truck. Adding insult to near injury, "F"#1 laid on his horn and hit his high beams, oblivious to the fact that *he* created the problem by pulling into another driver's blind spot.

PS—I labeled car #2 as an "F" because he, too, could have prevented this problem by glancing over his left shoulder in anticipation.

Now where did I put my "F" swatter?

⬙ The *Idiot*arod

In contrast to the world's foremost dogsled race—the Iditarod—I've actually found myself on an interstate highway going less than 20 mph in the snow, mushing along behind a team of "F"s in my own private *Idiot*arod. Being cautious is one thing, but this behavior is a bit extreme.

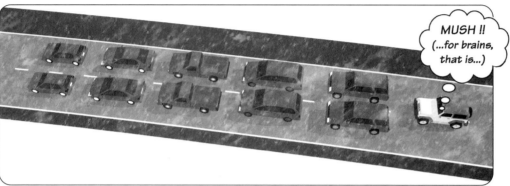

MUSH !! (...for brains, that is...)

Conversely, there are "F"s who drive at unsafe speeds simply because they have all-wheel drive (AWD). A little tip: AWD doesn't improve your ability to stop in the snow. In fact, the added weight of AWD mechanisms actually increases stopping distances. Braking in snowy conditions relates to tires, weight, and antilock braking systems . . . it has nothing to do with AWD.

BET YOU WISH YOU HAD ALL-WHEEL ... WHOA !

IDIOT...

Here's a related question: why do "F"s decelerate before going up a snowy hill? This is completely counterintuitive. Intelligent drivers know to *gain* momentum before hitting an incline in order to facilitate getting up and over it without slipping. Slowing down is the proper course of action before heading *down* a snowy hill, not the other way around.

And when "F"s feel themselves losing traction, they massively overcorrect by sawing their steering wheels back and forth in a frenzied manner. Another tip: once a snow tire is no longer rolling in the same direction as the vehicle, it loses most of its grip. At that point, it won't do much to facilitate steering *or* stopping. The proper method is to steer smoothly and consistently *into* the direction of travel when starting to skid.

Finally, *always* check conditions periodically when driving in the snow. When it is safe to do so, test how hard your brakes can be pressed before losing traction. This information will come in handy when it's really needed.

Before we leave snow country, I'd like to impart one final message: When alternate-side-of-the-street parking is in effect, obey the rules. Violators should prepare to get plowed . . . by the **"F"-INATOR!**

 # You Never Played Sports, Did You?

I hold the following truths to be self-evident:

> People who study harder receive better grades.
> Those who work harder enjoy more successful careers.
> Those who train harder become better athletes.

While I do believe that all people are (for the most part) created equal, experience indicates that hard workers rise above the rest.

Larry Bird is a classic example. He happened to be tall enough to play basketball, and he was also blessed with incredible hand-eye coordination and peripheral vision. But he couldn't jump, he wasn't fast, and he wasn't especially strong. So how did he become one of the best talents the NBA has ever seen? He *worked* at it. He studied the game incessantly and he practiced hard. His career and life are admirable, and for the most part he accomplished what he did without anyone's help but his own.

What does that have to do with road rage? Well, this "F"-isode exposes those who never studied, trained, or worked hard.

In heavy traffic on a four-lane divided highway, a slug like the one shown below will inevitably hog the left lane. "F"s who decided to skip sports or who played but never practiced are less coordinated than the rest of us. When they dilly dally in the left lane, they don't closely follow the vehicle in front of them because their spatial perception is off, and therefore they don't trust their own reflexes.

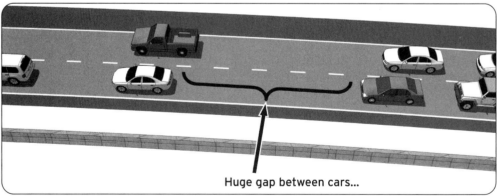

Huge gap between cars...

As a result, vehicle after vehicle slides in from the right as an "F" like this single-handedly turns the fast lane into the slow lane.

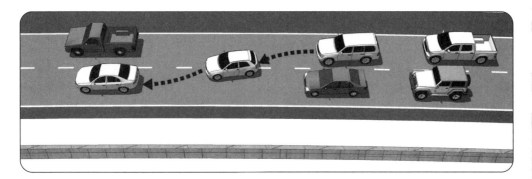

Speaking of sports, these "F"s are the type of parents who believe that there should be no winners and losers when kids compete, that scores shouldn't be kept, and that kids shouldn't be allowed to choose sides for fear that their own child's feelings might be hurt. Give me a break!

When we (in Class A) were kids, we learned at an early age that the harder we tried the better we performed. *That* was what kept us from being chosen last. And losing a game motivated us try harder so we wouldn't lose *again*.

"F"s, on the other hand, shelter their children from the "massive psychological trauma" of losing a game or being chosen last, thereby preventing them from learning these critical life lessons. Consequently, the rest of us are forced to suffer through generation after generation of emotionally challenged morons.

More fodder for why I apply pass/fail grading (and win/lose thinking) to the human race.

⊕ PITA in the HOV Lane—OMG!

HOV (High Occupancy Vehicle) lanes were created to *save time*, which occurs unless there's a PITA (Pain in the Ass, a.k.a. "F") involved. By consciously deciding to take along a passenger, Class-A drivers can use HOV lanes to arrive at their destinations sooner and thus accomplish more. The fact that these lanes are located to the left of the main highway also infers that they were intended to be *fast* lanes. And since HOV lanes are usually bordered by wide median strips, maintaining healthy speeds is rarely a problem. There's even an attendant benefit of a reduction in fuel consumption due to carpooling.

COME ON ! MOVE IT, MORON !!

Driving with my wife one day on a busy weekend, we entered an HOV lane. Shortly thereafter, we pulled up behind a PITA who was in that lane traveling below the speed limit. Even with heavy traffic, the three lanes to our right were outpacing us. So instead of saving time, this "F" was now *costing* us time.

Not good.

As the miles passed, a line of vehicles piled up behind us. Some of them became frustrated to the point of illegally crossing over the median strip to rejoin the primary traffic lanes. I decided not to follow suit because the median strip was full of debris and I didn't want to kick any of it up onto my car or others' cars.

My wife and I happened to be headed to a medical appointment that day and didn't want to be late, so we decided to get off at the next exit and take the back roads.

As I accelerated into the exit lane, I realized that the "F" was traveling so slowly that there was actually room to move back into the HOV lane in front of him. So I did.

Does anyone want to guess what happened next? Yes, that's right . . . he flashed his high beams.

I try to imagine what goes through the mind of an "F" when he does this. The obvious answer? Nothing . . . nothing at all.

Men at Work

The PROBLEM:

In heavy traffic, a car abruptly darted from the right lane into the middle lane, caus-ing me and others to hit our brakes.

The CAUSE:

An "F" saw a work crew up ahead and "instinctively" moved to the left.

Work truck on shoulder

"F" darting to the left

UNNECESSARY, MORON.

"F"'s need to know that I intentionally put "instinctively" in quotation marks because they don't *have* proper instincts. You see, for obvious reasons, work crews aren't actually allowed to park on the highway. No . . . they're instructed to park on the shoulder . . . that area to the *side* of travel lanes.

But just as a dog can't help but chase a stick, "F"'s immediately cram themselves into an adjacent lane the minute they see something up ahead on the right.

Woof.

Steering from the Rudder

In contrast to the grandstanding you'll see from flamboyant, highly visible CEOs, "steering from the rudder" is a management term used to describe executives who run their companies from behind the scenes.

"F" matching my speed and blocking traffic

Let's apply this concept to the road. If you're in Class A and happen to not be in a hurry on a particular day, you'll be traveling in the right lane to be courteous. And since "F"s are everywhere, one will invariably come up alongside you in the left lane and match your speed.

When this happens, do what I do:

THANK YOU !!

YOU'RE WELCOME.

Either slow down and make the "F" pass you . . .

. . . or accelerate so your buddies in Class A have room to pass him on the right.

DITTO !

NO PROBLEM.

In any event, you can still fix the problem in the left lane by "steering from the rudder" in the right lane.

(Unfortunately, you can't expect CEO-level compensation for this magnanimous act . . . sorry.)

EXIT 3

The Importance of an Exit Strategy

A "strategy" can be defined as a plan, method, or series of maneuvers used to achieve a specific goal or result. In this book, the term "exit strategy" signifies the use of such a plan or method when approaching a highway exit. Class-A drivers recognize the importance of having an exit strategy, whereas "F"s never do.

Take this EXIT to see how "F"s lose all sense of reason when they're about to miss a turn. I'll teach you how to turn over a new cloverleaf. Then our old friend Snagglepuss will remind us how to "exit . . . stage left" (and right).

✚ Will the World Come to an End If You Miss Your Turn?

I can't tell you the number of times I've seen "F"s realize at the last minute that they were about to drive past their exit (. . . or turn . . . or store parking lot . . . or whatever). They slam on the brakes and turn wildly to avoid going by, unable to process the concept that they could just turn around and double back. And since they've been driving along oblivious to their surroundings, "F"s never envision the consequences of their abrupt maneuvers. Here are a few I've seen:

(1) An "F" slammed on his brakes to enable a right turn onto a cross street. Several vehicles, including mine, were forced to screech to a stop. No accident but close.

(2) Another "F" hit his brakes and abruptly turned into a McDonald's entrance. In this case, a boy was riding his bicycle down the sidewalk and he crashed right into the "F." One second later and the kid might have been run over!

Why We Feel "Road Rage" . . . And Why It's Your Fault!

(3) An "F" veered across *two* highway lanes at the last minute, causing an SUV in the center lane to swerve into a car traveling in the right lane.

You know, even in my imagination, I realize that the **"F"-INATOR** wouldn't be able to handle every problem without help. So I also envision booby traps that would automatically spring into action when "F"s misbehaved . . . like this huge exit-ramp pinball flipper . . .

 Pick a Lane . . . Any Lane

Although this "F"-isode displays another instance of the need to impede, I've included it here since it specifically relates to "exit strategies."

> PICK A LANE, "F"!

Far more often than not, an "F" will hug the center line on a two-lane exit ramp. Sometimes this must be rooted in his lack of confidence that he could successfully navigate either lane without bouncing off the guardrail. More likely, though, it stems from his need to seize control of another person's time, even if only for a moment.

Depending on my mood, I may sympathize with the poor sap. Usually, though, I'll blow by him once he leaves enough wiggle room, and then . . . wait for it . . . waaaait for it . . . he'll flash his high beams in protest. Yes, the very same idiot who caused the problem is now attempting to punish the innocent. What a complete and utter moron.

I wonder what I should do the next time I run across an "F" in this situation . . .

. . . I guess I'll burn that bridge when *he* comes to it.

May the Centrifugal Force Be with You

Some exit ramps are designed (by "F"s) with far too tight a turning radius. Most ramps, however, have an appropriate balance of length, slope, and curvature.

So here's a notice to Mr. and Mrs. "F": when you round an exit ramp, you don't have to slow down to a crawl.

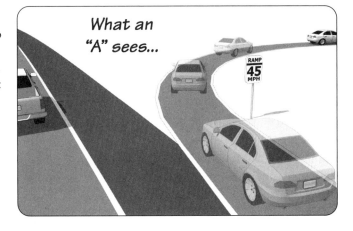

You see, tires are made of this substance called *rubber* . . . which is *sticky*.

You can actually maintain a reasonable speed through a turn without flipping over and bursting into flames.

Although I'd cope . . .

⬦ Turning Over a New Cloverleaf

There's a part of my daily commute where a six-lane divided highway crosses over a two-lane highway, forming a "cloverleaf." Both roads are extremely busy during rush hour. Our three lanes tend to back up for miles leading up to this cloverleaf, while the highway beyond it is free of congestion. To demonstrate why this occurs, I've grouped together several common blunders made by "F"s in this situation.

Blunder #1: continuing to travel in the right lane through a cloverleaf, even though they're not exiting.

Let's see . . . vehicles are exiting *from* and merging *into* the right lane, but "F"s continue to travel *in* that lane? Uh huh . . . very smart.

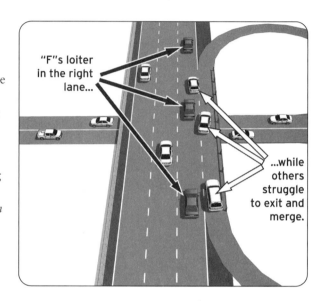

"F"s loiter in the right lane...

...while others struggle to exit and merge.

Blunder #2: not moving into the proper lane as soon as they're able.

When "F"s exit, they don't move from the right lane into the exit lane until the very last minute, and vice versa when they merge onto the highway.

This dope, who's merging, should be in the travel lane already...

...and this one should be in the exit lane by now.

Blunder #3: not timing their exit with another vehicle's merge.

As an "F" approaches a cloverleaf, he fails to anticipate where his vehicle will synch up with others.

If an "F" is also driving the merging vehicle, he won't have anticipated this merge either.

So now the two idiots become simultaneously surprised by the situation that they've been "suddenly" thrust into.

Each of these examples results in every commuter's worst nightmare: the use of brake lights. Once that starts, the herd mentality takes over. Every "F" on the highway hits their brakes in a reflex move, causing a chain reaction that backs up traffic for miles, as indicated earlier.

So, "F"s, why don't you admit your failings and try turning over a new leaf?

⟨ Exit . . . Stage Left

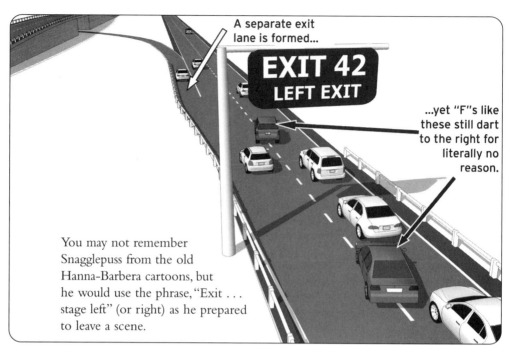

A separate exit lane is formed...

EXIT 42
LEFT EXIT

...yet "F"s like these still dart to the right for literally no reason.

You may not remember Snagglepuss from the old Hanna-Barbera cartoons, but he would use the phrase, "Exit . . . stage left" (or right) as he prepared to leave a scene.

Well, in a city near my home, there are several "Left Exits" from a highway. Notice that I didn't say "Left-Lane Exit Only" . . . no, just "Left Exit."

When "F"s see a sign for such an exit, they invariably panic and dart into the right lane. They give no consideration to whether or not there is already someone *in* the lane next to them; instead they mindlessly stuff themselves in.

This is moronic, rude behavior and is due to a relatively minor case of misapplied Boolean logic (the science of if-then statements). An extreme case is covered in the "F"-isode titled "All Dogs Are Mammals, but Not All Mammals Are Dogs" (see EXIT 12).

It's amazing that "F"s like these were able to pass their driving exams in the first place, although I suppose those particular exams could have been *graded* by "F"s. (There's got to be a double-negative buried in there somewhere . . .)

Exit . . . Stage Right

One of the rare times that "F"s actually put a smile on my face is when they pull into exit lanes too *early*. The diagram below depicts an actual stretch of road near my home. Here's what happens:

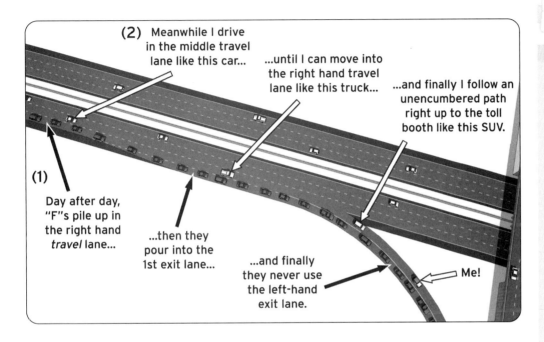

(2) Meanwhile I drive in the middle travel lane like this car...

...until I can move into the right hand travel lane like this truck...

...and finally I follow an unencumbered path right up to the toll booth like this SUV.

(1) Day after day, "F"s pile up in the right hand *travel* lane...

...then they pour into the 1st exit lane...

...and finally they never use the left-hand exit lane.

← Me!

To ensure that my life remains balanced, however, "F"s also do just the opposite, routinely slowing down well *before* they've reached an exit ramp.

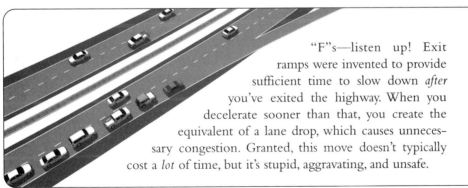

"F"s—listen up! Exit ramps were invented to provide sufficient time to slow down *after* you've exited the highway. When you decelerate sooner than that, you create the equivalent of a lane drop, which causes unnecessary congestion. Granted, this move doesn't typically cost a *lot* of time, but it's stupid, aggravating, and unsafe.

Am I "right"?

Mastering the Fine Art of the Merge

Merging can be defined as two vehicles "blending together gradually" ... "intermingling smoothly" ... "fitting harmoniously." Not exactly what you'd call "F" language, now is it?

In this EXIT, Aesop's fable about the tortoise and the hare is exposed as utter nonsense. I'll also demonstrate how Pavlov's study of conditional reflexes in dogs applies to moronic drivers. Finally, you'll learn that cold cuts are more than just sandwich meats.

Slow and Steady Wins the Race?

This title comes from one of Aesop's fables ("The Tortoise and the Hare"), in which a tortoise who plodded along slowly won a race against a hare who sprinted ahead and tired himself out. Well, kids, that's not how it works in the real world. Steady, maybe. But slow? . . . uh uh. Here's one of Allan's axioms which is actually useful: always merge onto a highway *at speed*.

Virtually every vehicle on the road today has sufficient power to achieve highway speeds by the end of an entrance ramp. Unfortunately, many vehicles also come equipped with "F"s. When they enter a highway traveling well below the speed limit, a temporary lane-drop is created.

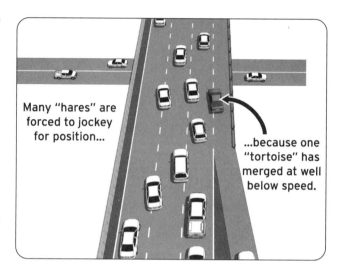

Many "hares" are forced to jockey for position...

...because one "tortoise" has merged at well below speed.

WHAT'S YOUR HURRY? LIFE'S TOO SHORT...

YOURS SURE IS !

Another real-life version of the tortoise vs. the hare . . . want to guess who comes out ahead?

Slow and steady wins the race? No . . . Aesop was an idiot.

Wait . . . Then Hurry Up and Wait

I was driving along one day, minding my own business and traveling slightly over the speed minimum as is customary. Traffic was very light. A vehicle up ahead was preparing to pull out from a side street.

My peers in Class A have all been down this road before, so they know what went through my mind—"Don't do it . . . doooon't doooo iiiiit." But as usual, *just* before I reached him, the "F" pulled out quickly and then proceeded to drive slowly.

So let's recap:

(A) He didn't pull out right away, but instead waited for me to get close:

= **WAIT**.

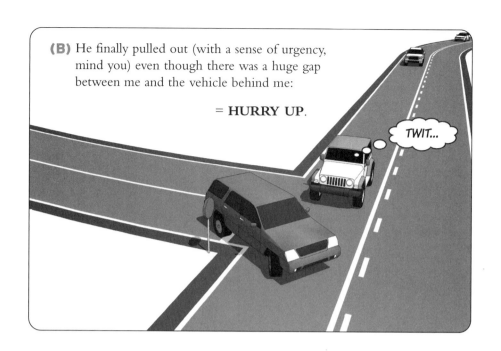

(B) He finally pulled out (with a sense of urgency, mind you) even though there was a huge gap between me and the vehicle behind me:

= **HURRY UP**.

TWIT...

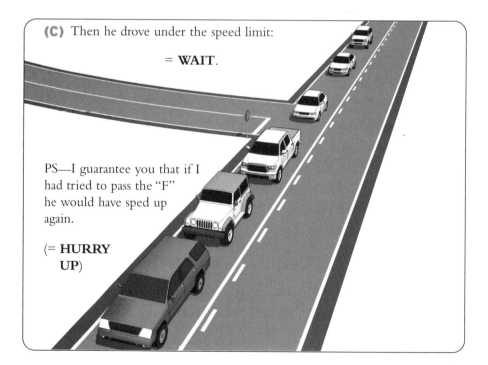

(C) Then he drove under the speed limit:

= **WAIT**.

PS—I guarantee you that if I had tried to pass the "F" he would have sped up again.

(= **HURRY UP**)

This "F"-isode demonstrates another common char-"F"-teristic: a lack of consistency. It makes me want to cry out to the "F"s, "Make up your tiny little mind, will you?"

Hold on a minute!   What's that noise?   Can it be?

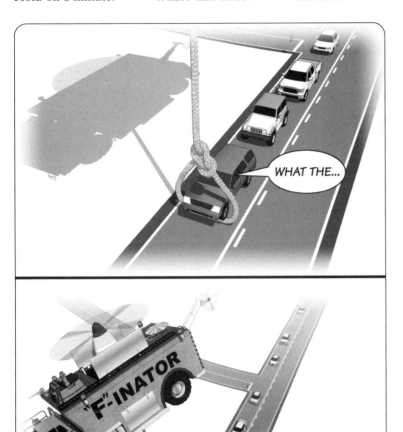

Well, of *course* the **"F"-INATOR** can fly!

 Pavlov's Dogs

Ivan Pavlov was a Russian scientist who first discovered the phenomenon known as "conditional reflexes." His work involved the measurement of salivation in dogs as they responded to external stimuli (i.e., a ringing bell, which had previously signaled the arrival of food).

"F"s display similar preconditioned responses on the road, as they are unable to simultaneously process more relevant, parallel information.

In one example, I was driving in the left lane on a four-lane divided highway, trailing an "F" who was in the right lane (for once). He noticed someone merging from the right and "instinctively" pulled into my lane and cut me off.

But this time the car was driven by a Class-A cohort who was merging at speed, which meant that the "F" pulled into my lane for literally no reason.

This member of Class-A had merged at speed...

...but this "F" cut into the left lane anyway.

When canine-brained "F"s like this see a vehicle merging, they immediately pull into the left lane, with no concept of how fast the merging vehicle is traveling . . . no thought or judgment is brought to bear. No, all they have is an animalistic reflex to external stimuli.

Never mind dogs . . . laboratory *mice* show better instincts than these lug nuts.

Now let's review another irrational sequence of events set off by you-know-who:

I merged at 60 mph onto a four-lane divided highway where an "F" was traveling at the same speed as I was in the left lane.

As I pulled into the right lane, I imagined him recalling a distant memory—he once was told that the left lane was known as the *passing* lane.

The "F" was traveling at 60 mph...

...while I merged at 60 mph.

He accelerated to at least 80 mph...

...as my cruise control pulled me to 75 mph.

As a result, a little robot voice in his head probably whispered, "I—am—in—the—left—lane—therefore—I—must—pass—that—Jeep."

As I gained speed, his "programming" told him to continue accelerating until he had successfully completed the pass.

He then moved back into the right lane (otherwise known as the slow lane) and his primitive instincts urged him to slow back down.

Bad doggy!

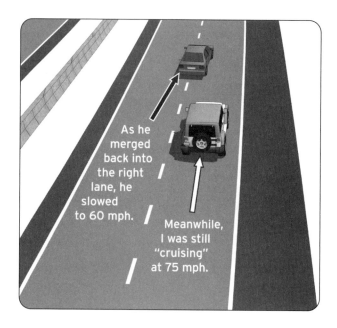

As he merged back into the right lane, he slowed to 60 mph.

Meanwhile, I was still "cruising" at 75 mph.

HURRY UP AND WAIT...

Now I had to pass *him*...

...because he was going 60 mph again!

I was finally forced to pull into the left lane to pass *him* (with my cruise control *still* set at 75 mph) because he had slowed once again to 60 mph.

I'd flowchart this inane decision making, but I care too much about the environment to waste that much paper.

Pavlov Also Had a Cat

In this "F"-isode, I
merged onto a
highway where an
"F" was traveling in
the *right* lane. The
left lane was totally
clear so he easily
could have moved
over . . . but he didn't.

If I hadn't hit my
brakes, I certainly
would have rubbed
him the wrong way.

Wide open
lane...

...but the "F"
refused to
take it...

...so I had to
hit the brakes!

You may wonder why this "F"-isode has "Cat" in the title.
It's because a dog would always obey the rules, whereas a cat
might not bother to change lanes. Why "Pavlov" again?
Because, as in the last "F"-isode, this "F" had to be conditioned to make this move too. I guarantee you that his
parents raised him to believe that he had as much right to
the lane as anybody else. "F"s beget "F"s.

Time for this "F" to be impounded . . .

HERE KITTY !

⟨↕⟩ It's Mine and You Can't Have It

I believe I was about six years old the last time I said something as childish as, "It's mine and you can't have it." "F"'s, though, never seem to lose this mindset.

Me hitting my brakes because of the dope in front of me.

When exiting a toll booth, I'll inevitably pull in behind a "child" who's slogging down the entrance ramp. He'll usually become fixated on what *I'm* doing, as evidenced by constant glances into his rearview mirror.

Because he's going so slowly, I and others behind me can't help but crowd him. I understand that this does little good, but it's *very* hard to give an "F" his space.

Once we reach the highway, I'll punch it and head toward the middle lane.

I take off to get around the putz.

Teacher: "Okay, class . . . what happens next? Oh, yes, Tommy, go ahead."

Tommy: "The guy in front of you pulls into the middle lane and cuts you off?"

Teacher: "Verrrry gooood, Tommy. Anything else?"

Tommy: "Oh!! Oh!! And there's no one in the right lane!"

Teacher: "Thaaaat's right. He only pulled into the middle lane to be difficult. Now class, what do we call people like that?"

Class: " "F"s!!"

Teacher: "Excellent! I'm so proud of you . . . you're all becoming good little "A"s!"

 # Cold Cuts

This "F"-isode finds me on a highway approaching an entrance ramp. I had pulled into the right lane about a mile back to let a tailgater go by, but he turned out to be an "F" and therefore *didn't* go by. Instead he matched my speed, trapping me in the right lane.

PLEASE PASS THE MAYO...

YIELD

"F" sandwich

Next, another "F" came to the end of the entrance ramp and pulled into my lane without hesitation. He didn't slow down . . . didn't observe the yield sign . . . didn't look in the mirror . . . didn't turn his head. Nope, he just kept coming.

So I found myself wedged between these two twits like a slice of baloney.

Don't you agree that it's "cold" when someone "cuts" you off like that?

Now that's got to be the best pun since sliced bread! Doesn't cut the mustard, you say? Well, maybe I need to slow down until you catch up. I've tried to stop being such a ham, but puns are my bread and butter. Maybe I should quit cold turkey?

Rotary Public

New England is home to these wonderful contraptions called rotaries, where usually four or more roads converge into a circular rotary (or roundabout) at the center. "A"s are able to think "outside the circle" and anticipate what will happen if more vehicles enter a rotary than leave it. Duh! We will only enter (see the white arrows) if we won't impede vehicles already *in* the rotary.

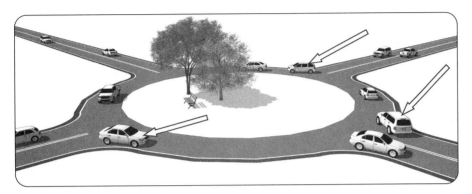

"F"s, on the other hand, invoke what they mistakenly believe to be their right-of-way by plowing headstrong into a rotary (see the black arrows). As more and more "F"s follow suit, every rotary will inevitably come to a stop, in essence creating circular gridlock, as depicted below. (I picture these same "F"s at home pouring more water into their dinner guests' glasses even though they're already full.)

Yo, "F"s—please, for once, pay attention—the "right" in "right-of-way" connotes *propriety* not direction. Having the right-of-way doesn't mean people on the right always go first!

You know, I feel like we've come full circle without you "F"s having learned a thing . . .

Left . . . Left . . . Left-right-left

As in the military march for which this "F"-isode is named, order and discipline are of primary importance. When merging from two lanes down to one, the commonly accepted rule is *every other vehicle*.

Exiting a toll booth is a classic example. One vehicle merges from the left, the next from the right, and so on. Traffic flows along quite nicely.

Every other car...a nice little custom.

"F"s stuffing themselves in just to be difficult.

REAL SMART...

But I suspect you've all seen "F"s who try to break this logical pattern by cutting off others. You might think that these particular "F"s are in a hurry, but more likely their only goal is to bring a speck of control into their sorry existence. All it takes is one or two jerks like this to turn a toll booth plaza into a parking lot.

The *only* time the every-other-vehicle rule may be broken is when a Class-A team member sees that an "F" has left too much room in front of himself. We're allowed to fill this gap without it being viewed as discourteous because it actually facilitates the flow of traffic.

It's time to send these "F"s back to basic training (a.k.a. "give them the boot" camp).

⊕ Lane Closed Ahead

I found myself stuck in a highway construction zone the other day, having just gone past an exit. A sign read, "Left Lane Closed 1 Mile," and upon seeing this, "F"s had immediately begun cramming themselves into the right lane, which caused a backup for almost an entire mile. More herd mentality.

I continued driving down the left lane until it was *actually* time to merge, at which point I selected a safe opening and pulled on over.

Even though there was ample room to merge and no one was cut off, I was still treated to a wondrous display of horn honking and high beams.

By refusing to merge a full mile before it was necessary, I'll admit that I gave the *appearance* of being rude. But I was not . . . I was simply being efficient.

If the world consisted only of Class-A drivers, everyone would continue to use *both* lanes until a lane drop actually occurred. We'd then obey the every-other-vehicle rule and traffic would flow smoothly.

But whether in a lame attempt to be polite or due to a lack of coordination (or maybe due to possessing the intellect of a tree stump), "F"s almost always merge prematurely. They jam themselves into the right lane while "A"s sail down the left lane; therefore, conflict is predictably created at the merge point.

I could go on and on, but let me conclude with this message to the "F"s: you should always quit while *I'm* ahead.

⟨F⟩ The Sign Says *Yield*, Butthead

This "F"-isode illustrates another entrance ramp to a highway near my home, where far too often an "F" will cut me off as he drives blindly past a yield sign.

Why would he do this, you ask?

It's possible that he didn't notice the sign or that he simply ignored it. If that's the case, then he'd be an unobservant twit. It's also possible that he mistakenly believed he had the right-of-way since he was entering from the right, but as outlined in "Rotary Public," that would make him a moron. And it's further possible that he knowingly violated the yield, which would mean he's an offensive jerk.

In any event, this is another instance where I would call the upon **"F"-INATOR**.

Let's zoom out to understand why vehicles entering from the right are required to yield. In the first scene below, vehicles yield appropriately and traffic backs up from the right, but notice that no one's safety has been compromised as a result.

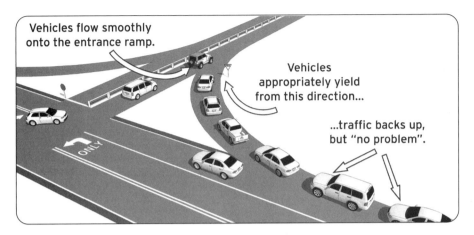

But when "F"s ignore the yield sign, vehicles entering the ramp from the left are forced to stop. Vehicles behind them crossing a lane of traffic are required to do the same, and therefore a safety hazard is created. The problem is compounded as traffic coming from the right is also held up.

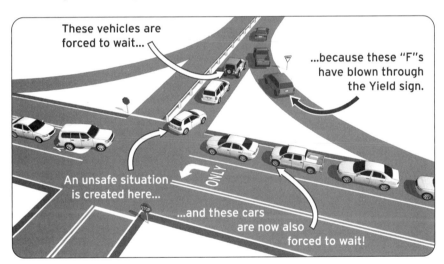

So, "F"s, listen up once again—"yield" indicates that you're supposed to give precedence to vehicles merging from the *other* direction. Only when there are no other vehicles merging are you allowed to proceed.

Are you following me? (You *should* be . . . that's the whole point!)

It's a *Yield* Sign, Not a *Stop* Sign

In contrast to the prior "F"–isode, there are situations where "F"s ineptly treat yield signs as if they're stop signs.

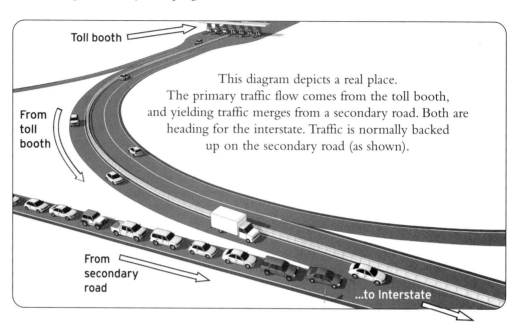

Toll booth

From toll booth

This diagram depicts a real place. The primary traffic flow comes from the toll booth, and yielding traffic merges from a secondary road. Both are heading for the interstate. Traffic is normally backed up on the secondary road (as shown).

From secondary road

...to Interstate

Let's walk through this . . .

The scene unfolds as an "F" approaches from the secondary road. The yield sign has rung his bell (hello again, Mr. Pavlov), telling him that he *must* yield.

His synapses continue to misfire, causing him to stop even though the sign says "yield."

Only *after* he's stopped does he crank his head over his left shoulder to evaluate when to proceed.

Having lost all momentum he now must wait as car after car creeps by at 30 mph.

Not until he sees a *huge* gap between vehicles will he finally proceed.

By this time, however, the damage has already been done.

What do those of us in Class A do instead?

We look left as soon as our field of vision allows . . .

. . . we pick a spot between two vehicles where we can merge without endangering anyone . . .

. . . and then we *time* our merge to allow that to happen.

No fuss, no muss.

Stating the Obvious

Here's another "F"-isode where the "F" Meter needle points directly to "Moron." I'll follow an "F" up an entrance ramp to a highway, and when we reach the end of the ramp, what does he do? Yep . . . he puts on his left turn signal.

Um . . . ya think? You see, I figured as much because, um . . . the entrance ramp is aimed left toward the highway and, uh . . . the ramp ends just up ahead and, duh . . . there's a guardrail on the right that you'd drive into if you *didn't* go left.

But thanks for signaling . . . very polite of you, dope.

Or how about "F"s who signal when they approach a one-way street?

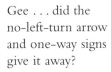

Gee . . . did the no-left-turn arrow and one-way signs give it away?

If only "F"s were this courteous and conscientious when it really mattered.

EXIT 5

To Everything...
Turn...
Turn...
Turn!!

The line above from the 1965 Byrds song is very appropriate because so many road rage emotions stem from the inability of "F"s to turn properly. "F"s neglect to go right on red when they're able. They inappropriately stick their vehicles' noses where they don't belong. Most don't leave enough room to go past them on the right when they take a left. Some even ignorantly wave other vehicles right into the path of oncoming traffic. A time to laugh . . . a time to weep . . .

✛ Wrong Turn on Red

I was driving through a green light when suddenly an "F" took a ~~right~~ wrong turn on red from the other direction. I was forced to swerve partway into the oncoming lane to avoid hitting him. Then the idiot had the nerve to honk his horn at *me*. Hey, moron, it's right on red only if there are no vehicles coming!

And now for a story that afforded me a rare, pleasant opportunity to observe road rage in an "F". I approached a traffic light behind an SUV. Across the intersection on the far-right corner was a gas station, which was my destination. There was little traffic.

Problem #1

As the idiot in front of me crawled along, I helplessly watched as the light changed from green to red.

Problem #2

He sat motionless in the right lane, blocking my right turn on red. I had previously assumed that he casually approached the light because he was taking a right at the light anyway. But no . . . he was a clueless "F".

So, realizing what was happening, I backed up, squeezed by him on the right (my tires actually catching the corner of the sidewalk), took my right on red, hung a left into the gas station, and started pumping.

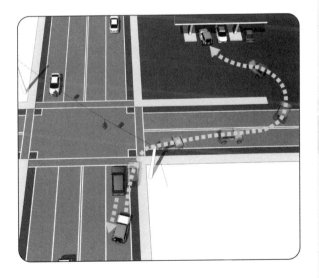

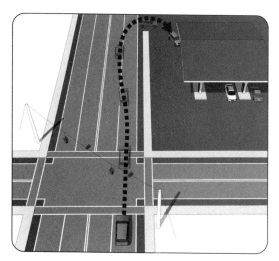

A minute later the light turned green, the idiot went straight through the intersection, and *then* he turned right into the gas station.

He pulled alongside the pump next to me, got out of his vehicle, and the following conversation ensued:

Him: (in a surprisingly shrill, whiny voice): "Hey mister, what's your hurry?"

Me: Silence.

Him: (louder, as if I didn't hear the fingernails on the chalkboard the first time): "Hey! What's your hurry?"

Me: I looked up this time, smiled, and said, "I really don't have time to ignore you right now."

Him: (after a dramatic pause): "Very funny. You know, you almost clipped my mirror on the way by just now."

Me: "The operative word being *almost*."

Him: "You should have just waited for the light to change."

Me: "No, *you* should have made a right turn on red instead of carelessly blocking the right lane. Try to do better next time."

Him: Silence . . . again.

Me: "Okay . . . I'm leaving now . . . but you have yourself a *great* day!"

As you can see, sometimes "F"s force you into it but don't engage them any more than you have to. Just ignore them as best you can and move on. They're not worth the energy.

My Way in the Driveway

How tough is it to back out of a driveway without holding people up? "F" behavior would lead us to conclude that it's damn near impossible.

To the "F"s I say, "Excuse me, pea brain, would you mind backing all the way across into your *own* stinking lane?"

Conversely, even "F"s wouldn't struggle to pull *into* a driveway, would they? Well, one day I witnessed an "F" pull into a McDonald's entrance, only to then stop for no apparent reason. A second "F" behind him had already begun to take a left across my lane without anticipating this possibility.

Surely you've heard the expression, "Two wrongs don't make a right." This "F"-isode proves that sometimes two "wrongs" can't make a left.

It Takes a Village . . . to Raise a Village Idiot

In the early years following the invention of the horseless carriage, automobiles had a very wide turning radius. In order to safely execute a right turn, drivers had to swing out wide to the left to avoid going into the oncoming lane *after* making their turn.

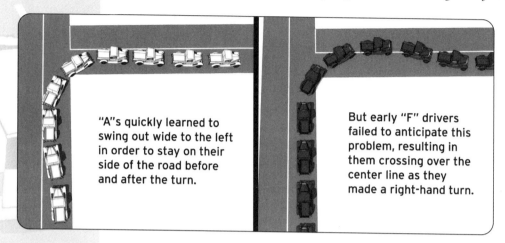

"A"s quickly learned to swing out wide to the left in order to stay on their side of the road before and after the turn.

But early "F" drivers failed to anticipate this problem, resulting in them crossing over the center line as they made a right-hand turn.

So how is it possible that this practice continues to this day even though nearly every modern automobile has a tight enough turning radius to negotiate *any* public road? It's because once "F"s finally learned this practice, they never *un*learned it.

MORON.

Generation after generation of idiot parents have continued to blindly teach their idiot children to swing out wide to the left because that's what *they* were taught. Worst of all, they swing out *too* far to the left, crossing over into the oncoming lane *before* their turn. This custom has continued for decades, long after technology has made such actions ridiculous.

Frequently an "F" will also neglect to signal during one of these wide turns. When followed by a second unobservant "F," that spells trouble.

And let's not forget to pay special attention when a big rig is making a turn, since they *are* still required to swing wide in most cases.

Here's my favorite bumper sticker of all time, which reminds us not only to give them ample room when turning but to always pass an eighteen-wheeler on the left as well.

Move Over, Red Rover

Okay, "F". I've pulled up behind you at a stop sign. You're taking a left, and I'm taking a right. Well, do you *think* you could move aside? No, you say? Not enough room? Or are you thinking, "Who does that guy think he is, wanting to drive by on the right?" (Oh, someone with things to do, that's all . . .)

Look, a minimum street lane width is normally about twelve feet. Although most shoulders are two- to four-feet wide, many secondary roads include no more than a one-foot shoulder before the curb. An average car's width is just over five feet, maybe six with mirrors. So, let's do some math together (back in school, I'm sure you "F"s felt that you'd never need math in the real world, but you were wrong, as usual):

Let's start with addition: 12' (lane) + 1' (shoulder) = ?

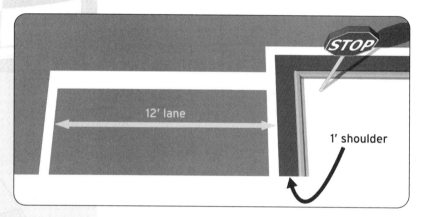

Yes . . .

13'.

Now we go to subtraction: 13' (lane + shoulder) − 6' (car width including mirrors) = ?

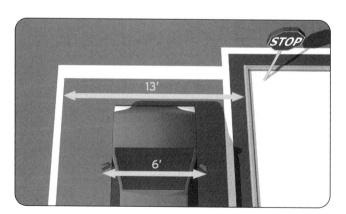

Hmm?

Okay, I'll answer this one for you . . . it equals 7'.

And now division:

$7' \div 2 = ?$

No, "F", it's not 72'.

It's 3.5'.

Or 3½' for those of you confused by decimals.

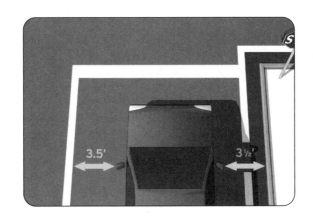

So . . . if you plop yourself in the middle of a lane at a stop sign or red light, that only leaves three and a half feet between you and the curb to your right. Therefore others can't proceed past you in their six-foot-wide cars.

All you need to do is hug the center line in order to let us by. Not hard.

And another thing:

When you're at a stop sign . . .

. . . and you *are* going right . . .

. . . would you please *go* already?

And last but not least—when someone does leave room for you to go by, would you please take advantage of this kind gesture and *make the damn turn*?

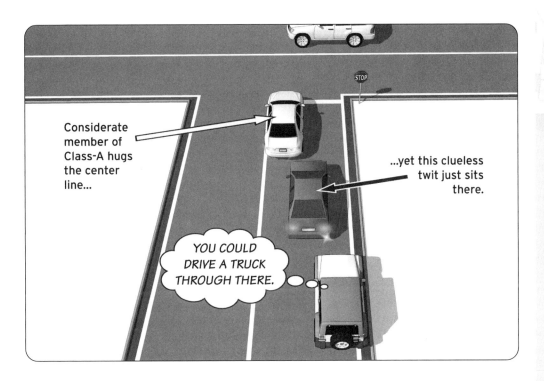

You're making me see red, rover . . .

. . . over!

◇Y◇ Go Left, Young Man

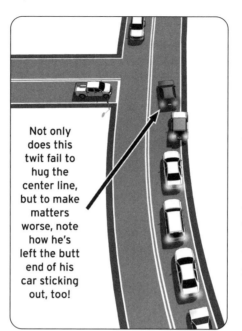

Not only does this twit fail to hug the center line, but to make matters worse, note how he's left the butt end of his car sticking out, too!

As explained in the previous "F"-isode, most streets are wide enough for two vehicles. But how many times before I'm dead must I sit behind an "F" as they prepare to take a left turn *without* leaving room for me to go by on the right? Worse yet, they stop after initiating the turn, which leaves the butt end of their vehicle sticking out even further.

Traffic backs up . . . time is wasted . . . road rage emotions smolder.

Another courtesy lesson (sigh) . . .

As previously outlined, cars average about five feet in width, six feet with mirrors, which means that with twelve feet of room two cars can pass each other.

Since roads are typically twelve feet wide with at least a two-foot-shoulder (fourteen feet total), that leaves *plenty* of room to spare between us if you'd only hug the center line.

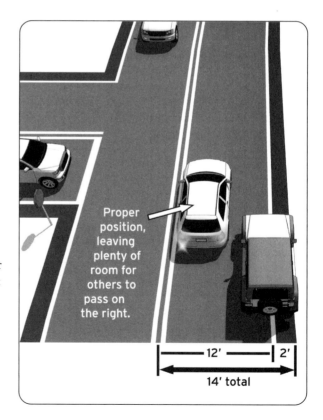

Proper position, leaving plenty of room for others to pass on the right.

12' — 2'

14' total

Some "F"s are now thinking (read this aloud with a whimpering tone), "But then I'd be crowding vehicles coming the other way!"

Well, audience, that whining sound means that it's time *once again* to play the new game show, "Twit or No Twit"!

A study was done (okay . . . *I* did the study . . . and if you think I'm kidding, consider how anal-retentive I must be to have written this book in the first place . . . so yes, I *did* a study!) where three separate two-lane roads were observed to measure how close to the center line people drove. My study included over fifty vehicles, and it confirmed what common sense had already told me (since sometimes it seems that there are fewer of us in Class A than in Class F, shouldn't ours be called

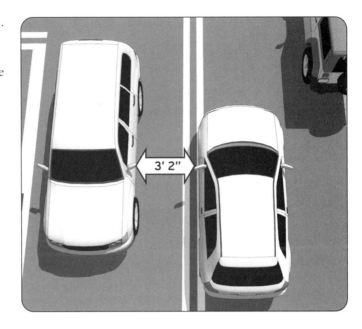

"uncommon" sense?). I digress . . . the study concluded that vehicles travel, on average, three feet, two inches from the center line. The closest measurement was two feet, one inch.

Now at this point I'm sure my colleagues in Class A are still with me, but "F"s are doubtless thinking, "What does *this* have to do with anything?" Well, go back one paragraph and it'll remind you that we were discussing the concept of hugging the center line to let others by. Even if you sit *right on* the center line, on average there will still be more than three feet between you and vehicles passing from the other direction.

So . . . when you go left, young man, would you please pretend you're a politician and hug the middle?

The Considerate Idiot

Sometimes idiots can be overly considerate. In the diagram below, you'll see that vehicles have backed up behind a slow-moving "F".

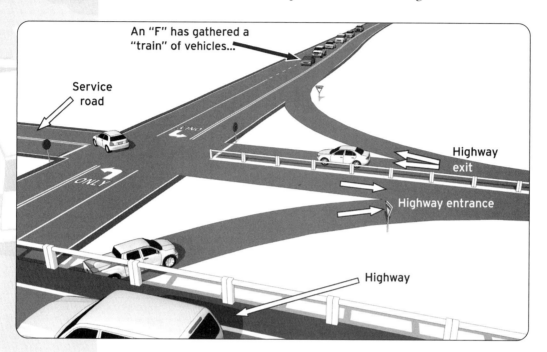

An "F" has gathered a "train" of vehicles...

Service road

Highway exit

Highway entrance

Highway

Now he and his "train" are about to take a left onto a highway ramp.

But what does he do? He flashes his lights and waves someone else on first! *Many* people now forced to wait while *one* person is allowed to go.

Where did I put my Tums?

This idiot waves to let one car go...

...holding up all of these people in the process.

There are so many things wrong with this move that I'm not quite sure where to begin. For starters, it violates a cardinal rule that the needs of the many outweigh the needs of the few.

Secondly, the person waiting to pull out never does so right away because never in his wildest dreams could he picture this idiot waving *him* on first.

So we all sit and watch as this scene unfolds in slow motion.

Finally, and worst of all, being universally oblivious to his surroundings, the "F" fails to observe whether or not there are vehicles passing him on the right and therefore will oftentimes wave *another* "F" right into the path of oncoming traffic! (An "A" would always wait until he knew the coast was clear.)

I've never actually seen an accident resulting from this gap in brain activity, but I've seen patches of rubber laid down in avoidance.

There is such a thing as being *too* considerate . . . idiot.

↯ The Le-"F"-t Turn

This guy signals...

...so the "F" waits.

PLENTY OF TIME TO TURN, MORON.

I pull up behind an "F" who's preparing to take a left turn. In this case, I'm also taking a left. Just before the "F" proceeds, a car approaching from the other direction puts on his right turn signal. Seeing this, the "F" stops and allows that person to go first.

What?

So let me get this straight, "F"—you're closer to the intersection and have ample time to safely complete your turn, but you give an approaching vehicle the right-of-way simply because he's engaged his turn signal?

While you let this guy turn...

...here comes another.

Great. So now I sit behind you in mental anguish as you wait for him to turn first. This delay allows more vehicles to approach from the other direction, which causes you to repeat the pattern . . . and suddenly I find myself in the movie, *Groundhog Day* . . . and suddenly I find myself in the movie, *Groundhog Day* . . . and suddenly . . .

Here's another related le-"F"-t: an "F" who fails to pull far enough into an intersection to prevent opposing cars from turning in both directions before him. In most cases this results in him (and me) becoming stranded at a red light because he didn't "reserve his ground."

Then there are twits who pull *too* far into an intersection. I was once behind an "F" who was so busy yapping on his cell phone that he drove almost completely through an intersection in which he had intended to take a left.

So what did I do? I safely pulled an inside move and made a left turn *behind* him.

I fully understand that a ticket could have landed in my lap had there been a cop around, but after making it this far into my book, I sure hope there's at least a *part* of you that feels the careless cell-phone yapper would have been more deserving.

Stop Sticking Your Nose into Other People's Business

You've already learned that students of Class A understand physics. Well, we have a firm grasp on geometry too. Depending on the circumstances, angles can dictate appropriate road conduct.

If he's slowing to take a left...

...then you have time to proceed.

One problem occurs when an "F" waits (and waits . . . and waits) to take a left turn at a stop sign. This illustration shows a road that comes to a "T" at a common 90-degree angle. Many times I've had my life put on pause as car after car took a left around an "F" even though he had sufficient time to proceed without incident.

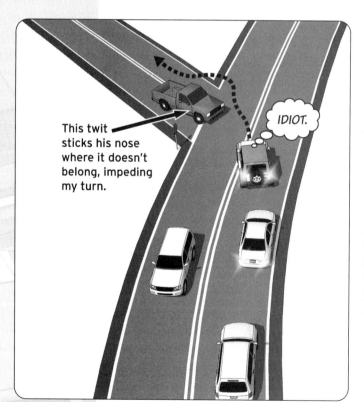

This twit sticks his nose where it doesn't belong, impeding my turn.

IDIOT.

The converse can be seen in a left turn that I take every night on my way home from work . . . it's not a typical 90-degree turn but more of a fork in the road. At this angle, traffic flow is best facilitated by yielding to vehicles making the turn since they're traveling at speed.

But "F"s didn't study in geometry class, and therefore they, like the angle depicted here, are *obtuse*. They carelessly creep too far forward, making it difficult (if not impossible) for others to sweep through the turn.

Hey, "F" . . . did the **"F"-INATOR** get your nose a little out of joint?

EXIT 6

Please...
I Beg You...
Make It Stop

A phrase I often scream as I'm jolted awake from road-related nightmares.

For some strange reason, "F"s are overly enthralled with stopping. Their behavior would indicate that it's quite possibly their favorite thing to do, because once they've stopped it takes them an inordinate amount of time to get moving again.

It's good advice to "stop and smell the roses" once in a while, but unlike "F"s, we "A"s realize that sometimes you can still smell those roses on the way by!

Two by Two at a Four-way

Once upon a time, some genius decided that the best practice at a four-way stop would be for vehicles in opposing directions to proceed through the intersection one at a time. Well, that genius was an "F". Not only does it take longer to go through one at a time, but oftentimes you'll find four idiots all politely waving to each other. "Go ahead." "No, you go ahead." "Oh no, after you."

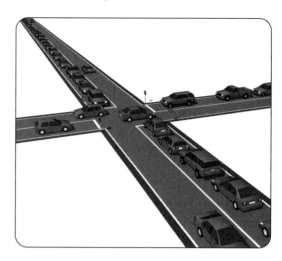

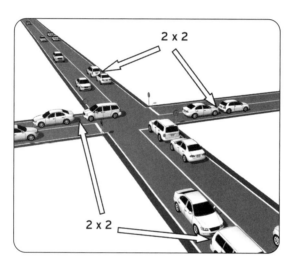

So from now on, we "A"s are going to proceed through *two* at a time, in tandem, allowing everyone to spend just about half the time at every four-way stop. The diagram to the left displays how this same intersection will appear once this new custom is adopted.

This won't create any problems and here's why:

(a) Those of us in Class A will appreciate the logic in this approach.

(b) Most "F"s won't know what's happening to them until it's too late.

(c) The few "F"s who *do* pay attention might flash their lights and beep their horns in protest, but we'll just ignore them . . . they'll catch on eventually.

The world will now be a more enjoyable place . . . "A"s will be happier and "F"s will be better off (although most won't even realize it).

What Part of "Go" Don't You Understand?

As previously mentioned, "F"s sure know how to stop, but they don't seem to grasp the concept of "go."

The diagram below depicts an area near my home. Here's what happens night after night after long, tiring night. At the end of this particular highway exit ramp, many of us need to take a left onto a street that is typically very busy. The ramp's left side always backs up for the following reasons:

(a) Some "F"s (who didn't play sports) wait until the road is virtually empty before they *dare* to pull out.

(b) Other "F"s (considerate idiots) hesitate to pull across someone's path because they're trying to be polite (of course, they're unknowingly being *im*polite to everyone on the ramp behind them).

(c) Other "F"s linger at the stop as they exercise patience. Whatever.

(d) Most importantly, the second "F" in line always sits there like a dope because it's "not his turn" yet. His linear-thinking bird brain tells him, "How could I possibly go when there's someone in front of me?" He waits until *after* the first person pulls away, then he pulls up to the stop, and *only then* does he bother to evaluate when to pull out.

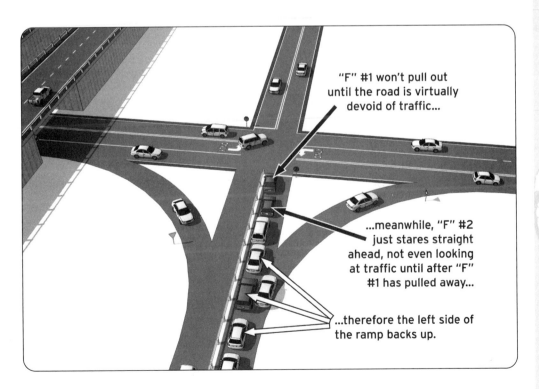

"F" #1 won't pull out until the road is virtually devoid of traffic...

...meanwhile, "F" #2 just stares straight ahead, not even looking at traffic until after "F" #1 has pulled away...

...therefore the left side of the ramp backs up.

From now on, people in Class A should do what I do:

I pull up alongside (but slightly behind) the first person at the stop sign, maintaining my line of sight in both directions. As he checks traffic, *I* check traffic.

When he pulls out, *I* pull out.

I swing out a little wide so that we cross into the travel lane concurrently, and off we go. Not a single person is delayed as a result of this maneuver, and I've saved time for every driver on the ramp behind me.

You're welcome.

Why We Feel "Road Rage" . . . And Why It's Your Fault!

Interestingly, even my Class-A brethren are initially surprised when they notice me there beside them, but once they see the logic behind what I'm doing they usually get a kick out of it. It's fun to actually partner with someone on the road for a change.

"F"s are, of course, another story. They act as if I'm trying to go *around* them, expressing their displeasure by sharing dirty looks and making flailing gestures with their arms, similar to those made by an ape when disturbed in its cage.

But whether I'm behind an "A" or an "F ", I go anyway. Another win-win.

A Chip off the Old Blockhead

This one blockhead creates misery for everyone around him.

Even an "F" can become impatient if he waits long enough, so this is what he'll sometimes do to enable a left turn across traffic. As his twit parents no doubt trained him to do, he'll pull out and block one lane while he waits for the other direction to clear.

Look, "F", if you're too uncoordinated to time two traffic lanes at once, then take a right and double back or else . . .

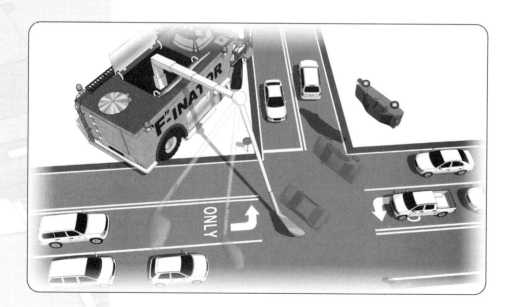

Nice chip, **"F"-INATOR!**

⟨↕⟩ Follow the Leader

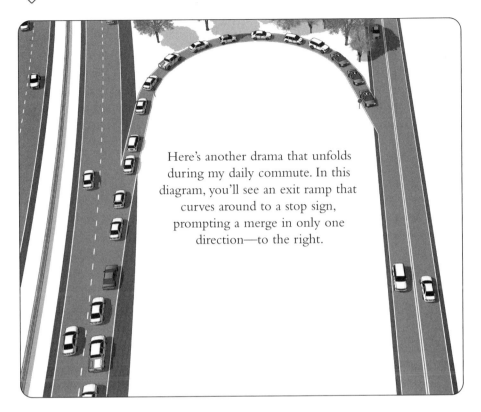

Here's another drama that unfolds during my daily commute. In this diagram, you'll see an exit ramp that curves around to a stop sign, prompting a merge in only one direction—to the right.

As depicted, highway traffic leading to this exit ramp is *always* backed up. Let's explore how a lack of "following the leader" creates this mess:

(a) "F"#1 initiates this chain reaction. As he takes the exit, his mental focus is restricted to the ramp itself. Being a linear thinker, he doesn't observe traffic on the street he's about to enter *while* he's still on the ramp.

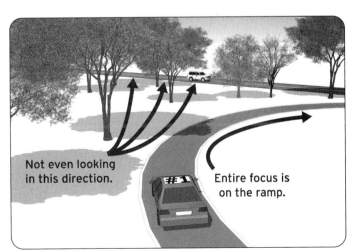

Not even looking in this direction.

Entire focus is on the ramp.

(b) He continues merrily down the ramp until he comes to a complete stop . . .

. . . and only *then* does he finally crank his head over his left shoulder to gauge whether or not he can pull away.

(c) While all this is going on, "F"#2 blindly follows "F"#1 down the ramp. Once he reaches the end of the ramp, he sits there staring straight ahead as he waits for "F"#1 to pull out.

Looking *only* here...

...not here.

THANK *GOD* HE'S FINALLY GONE. OKAY NOW...LET'S HAVE A LOOK SEE...

(d) Only *after* "F"#1 pulls out does "F"#2 pull up to the stop sign and finally look left to determine when *he* can pull out.

These steps are repeated by "F", after "F" causing a backup on the ramp as well as on the highway leading to it.

Instead, I do what others in Class A do, which saves time and therefore makes sense: as I proceed down the ramp, I observe the street ahead to see if there's any traffic. That way, by the time I reach the stop I've already determined whether or not I can proceed.

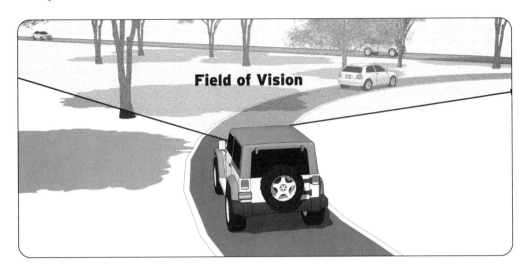

And when I'm in the second position, I *still* glance to the street in advance. Once I reach the stop, however, the person in front of me becomes my eyes. By looking at his head movements, I can effectively gauge the situation. When he pulls out, it will be safe to follow him 99 percent of the time, so when he goes, *I* go.

After I've started moving, I check my side-view mirrors to confirm that the road is clear before continuing. In the rare case when it isn't, I delay my merge until it is safe.

In any event, this approach allows *many* vehicles to pull away from the stop together, emptying the ramp more quickly and thereby eliminating congestion both on the ramp and back on the highway.

(And don't *even* get me started about tickets being handed out for rolling stops. Oh yeah . . . *there's* another social crisis we need to reel in!)

In conclusion, Class A consists of leaders. This "F"-isode demonstrates that "F"s, on the other hand, sometimes aren't even competent enough to be called followers.

✛ Dancing with the Cars

Have you ever witnessed this "tango" between a couple of "F"s? As one "F" pre-pares to take a left at a stop sign, another pulls up immediately alongside him to take a right.

Due to this lack of attention and common sense, now *neither* "F" can see past the other.

"F"#1 instinctively creeps forward in an attempt to see past . . .

. . ."F"#2 does the same . . .

. . . and so it goes until both vehicles are pro-truding into traffic. It's like watching a couple of idiots on a dance floor unable to decide who should lead.

Another lesson: instead of pulling right up alongside another vehicle, why not hang back so you can see over the other guy's trunk?

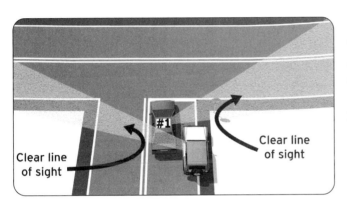

That way you can *each* see in both directions and either of you can proceed independently of the other once traffic is clear.

Now come on . . . even you "F"s should be able to follow these simple dance steps . . .

A New School of Thought

Does this scene look familiar?

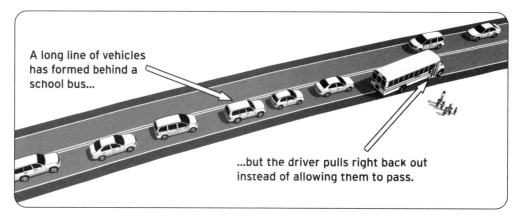

A long line of vehicles has formed behind a school bus...

...but the driver pulls right back out instead of allowing them to pass.

Once kids are off the school bus and out of harm's way, "F" bus drivers show a complete lack of courtesy by forcing us to remain behind them as additional stops are made. If they'd wait a mere fifteen seconds here and there, they could probably save each of us fifteen *minutes*.

Here's how the world should work:

In addition to those little stop signs that swing out when their doors open, school buses should all be equipped with "O.K. TO PASS" signs.

Bus drivers should be instructed (no . . . *required*) to use this feature once a line of vehicles forms behind them . . . *before* they pull back into traffic.

Don't you think I deserve an "A" for this idea?

⟨Ꮢ⟩ I'd Get by with a Little Help from My F-riends

What do you do when I look for some room, you refuse to accommodate me
Yes, it appears, you're a stupid buffoon, you're as ignorant as you can be
Oh, why can't I get a little help from my F-riends . . .

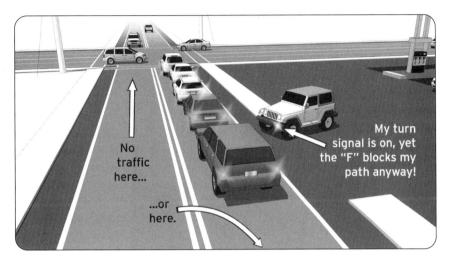

No traffic here...

...or here.

My turn signal is on, yet the "F" blocks my path anyway!

Okay, pay attention, "F"s. When idling in a line of vehicles, it costs you nothing to allow others to pull out.

If you don't, maybe you'll get "high" with a little help from *my* friend.

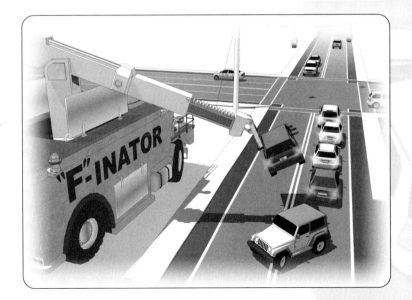

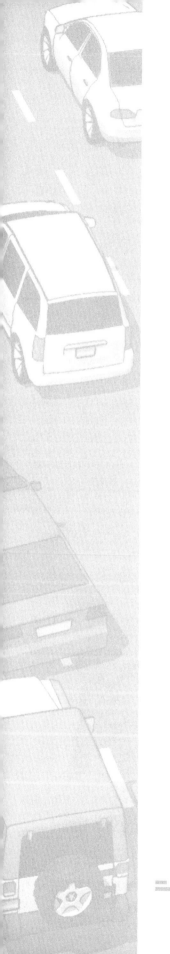

Let There Be Light

*T*his EXIT covers the use . . . or more appropriately the *misuse* . . . of lights. From interminable high beams to never-ending turn signals to confusion over the three little bulbs in a traffic light, "F"s constantly find ways to turn the sublime into the ridiculous.

 Are You High?

Hey, "F"s—turn off your stinking high beams when you're following me.

And turn them off when you approach me from the other direction too.

If I'm behind you on the highway, feel free to use your high beams. But once I pass you, off they go!

When idling on a roadside, turn off your headlights if you're pointed into traffic. Maybe you could even consider using hazard lights.

If your headlights are out of alignment and one of them is pointed too high, then guess what? Yep . . . it's become a high beam. If you plan to drive at night, please take it to a garage or fix it yourself.

Here's an idea—ask some friends for help . . . you know, to make sure you don't get in over your headlight.

(Now, that begs the question: how many "F"s *does* it take to change a lightbulb?)

One last item—a true caricature of "F" misbehavior:

An "F" will be headed toward you, having failed to turn off his high beams.

After briefly flicking your high beams as a gentle reminder, he turns his off.

Then he blasts you with his high beams at the last minute, just before driving past.

Once again, a guilty "F" somehow feels justified in punishing an innocent Class-A member. These are the same jerks who hog the left lane but then flip you the bird when you pass them on the right. I might actually feel contempt toward them if I could only muster the energy.

Asses to Asses . . . Dusk to Dusk

Who drives at dusk without putting on their headlights? Unobservant asses, that's who.

Okay, "F"s, allow me to once again explain something to you that is common sense to the rest of us: once it becomes dark enough for the first driver to turn on his headlights, most others will appropriately follow suit. They'll likely dim their rearview mirrors at the same time to prevent glare. In fact, many rearview mirrors dim automatically once hit by the first set of headlights.

Therefore, as you "F"s drive along mindlessly with your headlights off after others have already turned theirs on, you become an accident waiting to happen. You may still be able to see ahead, but you'll be nearly invisible in your fellow drivers' rearview mirrors.

So do us all a favor—when you see headlights, put yours on as well, okay, dimbulb?

⟨Y⟩ I'm Not a Mind Reader

I really love it when . . .

. . . an "F" slams on his brakes to turn . . .

. . . and *then* puts on his turn signal.

I also love it when . . .

. . . an "F" is heading toward me as I wait patiently at a stop sign . . .

. . . and then he suddenly makes a right turn *without* signaling.

Real nice.

And what's worse is when . . .

. . . an "F" is heading toward me with his turn signal *on* but doesn't turn until *after* he's gone by me.

Linear-thinking "F"s don't realize that this type of early signal could cause an accident.

Lucky for both of us I've paid attention all my life and therefore won't pull out until I know for sure where the other driver is headed.

But more than once I've seen an "F" signal prematurely, prompting *another* "F" to unwittingly pull out, neither of them having the foresight to prevent a collision.

It would seem that "F"s are not mind readers either.

Hey, you did a real bang-up job, "F".

Must have been that crash course you took.

⬧T⬧ Trump or No Trump?

I suspect that very few "F"s play bridge. This stands to reason since bridge is a game that requires logic, intuition, anticipation, and judgment. Once all fifty-two cards have been dealt, bridge players bid on the number of tricks they believe they can win. The winning bidder's partner then displays his cards face up on the table, and for this hand he becomes what is called the "dummy." (Hey, what do you know . . . maybe "F"s can be perfect bridge partners after all.)

Another key concept in bridge is the trump suit. Trump cards are sort of like wild cards. A lower card in the trump suit can beat a higher card in a suit that isn't trump. Are you following me, dummies? I didn't think so.

Anyway, you "F"s may now be asking, "What does this have to do with road rage?" Well, we "A"s often find ourselves impeded as one of you sits perplexed at a traffic light where the green left-turn arrow and the red bulb are *both* lit.

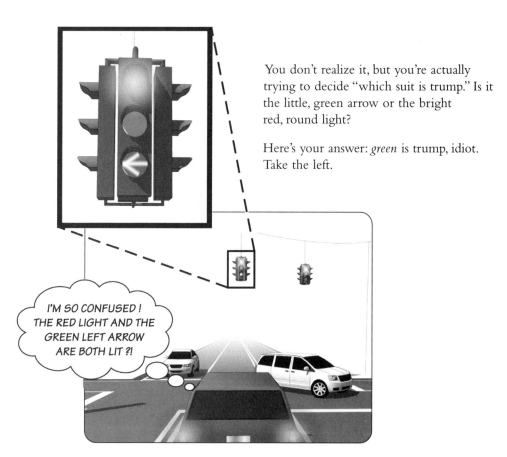

You don't realize it, but you're actually trying to decide "which suit is trump." Is it the little, green arrow or the bright red, round light?

Here's your answer: *green* is trump, idiot. Take the left.

I'M SO CONFUSED !
THE RED LIGHT AND THE
GREEN LEFT ARROW
ARE BOTH LIT ?!

The opposite condition can also be true, however, depending on which lane they're in.

Sometimes I'll be sitting behind an "F" in the right lane at a red light. The left arrow will turn green for the *left* lane and, practically every time this happens, the "F" in the *right* lane will proceed. The slightest glimmer of green combined with moving cars prompts him to instinctively hit the gas.

No, dummy, this time *red* is trump for your lane.

Clearly, driving is not something for which "F"s are well suited.

ⓨ The Never-Ending Story

POP QUIZ

Who leaves his turn signal blinking for miles on end with no intention of turning in the near future?

ANSWER

An "F" who's too brain dead to notice the incessant clicking sound or who can't be bothered to shut it off.

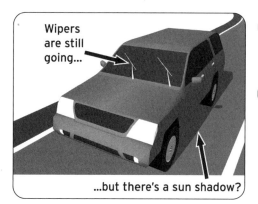

Wipers are still going...

...but there's a sun shadow?

QUESTION #2

Who leaves his wipers running after the rain has stopped?

ANSWER

Another "F" who doesn't notice as drying rubber scrapes and bounces across his windshield. (It must mimic the sound inside his empty head, so no wonder he doesn't notice. . . .)

BONUS QUESTION

Who caused wiper fluid to spray onto my windshield when I didn't activate my own wipers?

ANSWER

Yet another "F" whose wiper fluid nozzles are no longer pointing at his own windshield, so over the top it comes.

(Yes, I realize that this one could also be due to the slip-stream effect.)

Tunnel Vision

Most "F"s are afflicted with tunnel vision, a condition that flares up whenever they drive from broad daylight into a dimly lit tunnel. Because they neglect to remove their sunglasses, these dimwits' eyes can't adapt to the change in lighting conditions. They suddenly find themselves virtually blind, which results in the predictable, ridiculous reaction of hitting their brakes.

Whenever an "F" brags that he can always see light at the end of the tunnel, trust me—he's confused. What he means to say is that he can *only* see light at the end of the tunnel . . . because he's still wearing his sunglasses!

You've all heard of the tunnel of love? Well, you've now been introduced to the tunnel of loathe.

⬦ Understanding the Complexity of the Traffic Light

Okay, "F"s . . . this isn't that hard:

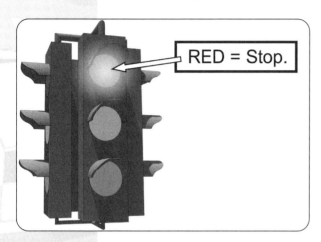

RED = Stop.

. . . running a red light is unacceptable under *any* circumstances!

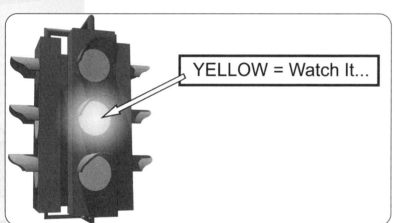

YELLOW = Watch It...

. . . time to slow down and play it safe.

(Note: You may only run a yellow light if you're *sure* you can make it through before the change to red.)

GREEN = Go !!

. . . as I asked earlier . . . what part of "go" don't you understand?

We in Class A never, *ever* want to see brake lights when approaching a green light (unless, of course, there's someone or something in the road ahead).

You "F"s should scurry along so we don't get stuck at a red light.

And if you're first in line when a red light turns green, would you please *go already*? Your mission should be to lead as many people through the light as possible. Stating the obvious, you say? Well, many a time I've been forced to sit through a second cycle because one of you dopes didn't proceed through a light in a timely fashion.

And here's another one:

There's a section of my commute where two traffic lanes pass through an intersection, after which the right lane veers off toward an interstate (my destination).

When the light at the intersection is red, at least one vehicle in the right lane always seems to be a tractor-trailer or tanker truck or some other "elephant." So normally I move into the left lane to avoid getting stuck behind it.

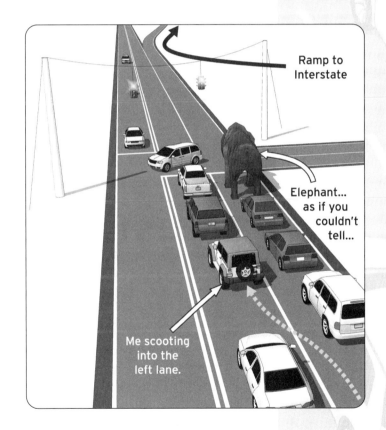

Then the *unthinkable* happens: when the light turns green, the lumbering rig actually out-accelerates an "F" who had also moved into the left lane in front of me.

"F" being outrun by the elephant !

This idiot...

...is completely responsible for this mess!

All of us who by now should have made it past the elephant must in this case jam ourselves into the right lane behind it, causing understandable grief to others already in that lane.

Once again, "F"s—green means *go*. This should be really easy for you . . . they both start with a "g."

Your Mother Must Be So Proud

I suppose *someone* has to land the job of programming traffic lights. It's not rocket science, I wouldn't think.

This "F"-isode exposes twits who program lights to change even when they're not tripped. There's one of these time-wasting signals in my town . . . I'll be driving along the main road minding my own business when out of the blue the light will turn red (no, "F"s . . . that doesn't make it purple). There's rarely anyone waiting to enter from the side street that receives the green . . . nope, the light changes to red all by itself.

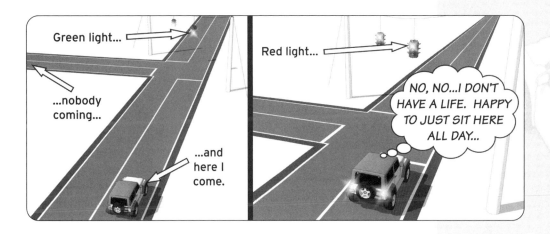

A brain only a mother could love . . .

Chain of Fools

Now for another rare "F"-isode where idiots actually *save* me time. This one happens just often enough to bait me into thinking that "F"s are finally starting to learn . . . you know, to stay out of my way.

It's pretty straightforward. I'll pull up to a red light and, to my delight, a chain of fools has formed in the right lane as if drawn together by a magnet. This leaves the left lane wide open for me.

I pity them . . . judge them . . . I berate them . . . but most of all . . .

I *sing* their praises . . . but just this once.

EXIT 8

Park Place
and
Bored Walk

"F"s hold a monopoly on bad behavior. One might argue that "A"s aren't perfect either, but here's another revelation: when "A"s let their emotions control their behavior, they temporarily *become* "F"s. It's been scientifically proven that members of Class A don't behave badly. It just doesn't happen.

This EXIT covers a myriad of parking indiscretions—"F"s who steal other people's spots, who walk directly in the path of vehicles trying to park, who take up two spaces by parking diagonally, who leave shopping carts in the spaces they've vacated, and who shamelessly park in handicap zones.

Yes, they indeed hold a monopoly and should "go directly to jail!"

Coloring Outside the Lines

Isn't it annoying when an "F" is too uncoordinated or careless to position his vehicle in the middle of a parking space? We've all returned to find some wing nut parked so close to our vehicle that we could barely open our door to get in. I'm sure these same "F"s were incapable of coloring inside the lines when they were children.

And we've all started to pull into a great parking space only to find that an imbecile has parked so far to the side of their adjacent space that *we'd* become an "F" if we tried to squeeze in.

So instead, Class-A heartbeats are needlessly wasted while looking for another spot. How wonderful.

Algebra in the Real World

Question: Why do "F"s take up two parking spots?

Answer: Because they only have half a brain . . . you do the math.

Let's see if the **"F"-INATOR** can solve this equation . . .

THAT'S WHAT YOU GET FOR PUTTING YOUR ASS ON THE LINE.

⟨↕⟩ Don't Mind Me

Oh, how I appreciate "F"s who back out of parking spaces without checking to see if another vehicle might be driving by. Very nice—thank you.

Although sometimes I'd rather they *not* look, because there are "F"s who intentionally take their sweet time whenever they see others waiting for their spots. (The need to impede strikes again.)

Why We Feel "Road Rage" . . . And Why It's Your Fault!

Then there are also times when you've been patiently waiting for a spot only to have an "F" steal it from you at the last minute.

Imagine the extreme joy you'd feel if you ever witnessed a cop ticketing an "F" for this move. Just picture it—an "F" steals your parking spot, gets out of his car, and is immediately confronted by an officer with a ticket pad. Wouldn't that be delightful?

Okay . . . wake up, everybody . . . dream over.

Is This Seat Taken?

What is it about certain people that makes it so hard for them to respect your space?

I can't tell you how many times I've returned to my car in an almost-empty parking lot only to find that an "F" has parked right next to me!

We meet these same people at the movies . . .

. . . and guys, we "meet" them at the ball game too, don't we?

The Cart Behind the Horse's Ass

Let's not forget slugs like the one shown below who are too lazy to return their shopping carts to the store once they're done with them.

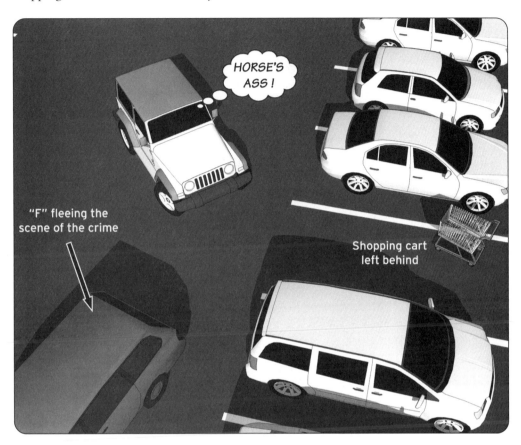

> HORSE'S ASS !

"F" fleeing the scene of the crime

Shopping cart left behind

No, instead we're required to get out of our car and move the cart before we can safely pull into the spot the "F" has just vacated.

By the way . . . don't bother shouting at them. You'll only get hoarse.

♦ Twits Family Robinson

Speech bubble: BUT OFFICER... MY FOOT SLIPPED... HONEST!

Disclaimer: no children were harmed during the formation of this daydream.

We've all found ourselves behind twits who refuse to politely move aside so we can proceed through a parking lot. They continue strolling along even when they're fully aware that we're behind them. Their children observe this behavior, ensuring that yet another generation of "F"s will carry on this tradition.

Speech bubbles: HEY! WATCH WHERE YOU'RE GOING, YOU @&#^$% !!

I TAKE IT YOU DIDN'T NOTICE MY BACKUP LIGHTS ?!

Another travesty happened to me just the other day. I had already begun backing out of a parking spot when an "F" walked directly into my path. He could have waited for a moment or walked around, but he chose to shout expletives at me instead.

(Don't waste your breath, "F".)

You can read about similar ironic (and moronic) behavior in the "F"-isode entitled, "Bull**** by the Horn," by taking EXIT 14.

What's *Your* Handicap?

I've never had the privilege of seeing a cop ticket someone for illegally parking in a handicap zone.

Sometimes I've seen "F"s do this to save time or effort.

At other times it's been a perfectly healthy person driving a vehicle with a handicap plate, but the handicapped person is not with them.

"F"s ought to be *slammed* for this kind of unconscionable behavior.

Well, at least struck by a meteor . . .

Why We Feel "Road Rage" . . . And Why It's Your Fault!

⟨⊢⟩ Linear Thinkers and Parallel Parking

Hey "F", if:

❱ my brake lights are lit;

❱ my turn signal's on;

❱ I'm not at an intersection;

❱ and there's on-street parking . . .

. . . then guess what? That's right . . . I'm parallel parking, so would you mind leaving room behind me so I can back in?

And if *you* intend to parallel park, please activate your turn signal. I'm incapable of reading a mind as miniscule as yours.

And last but not least are you jerks who rudely cut into my parking spot in a feeble attempt to improve your self-worth.

Pathetic.

EXIT 9

Road Warriors

Although this book was written for *everyone* who is frustrated by "F"s, there are several noteworthy subgroups whose struggles on the road make others' pale by comparison. These are our Class-A friends who are forced to navigate through the sea of "F"s as part of their daily jobs. I thought it appropriate to devote an entire EXIT to these road warriors.

Firefighters, paramedics, and police officers top the list. Quite literally, lives may be at stake when "F"s obstruct their paths. Next are parcel and mail delivery personnel whose very effectiveness depends upon their ability to arrive on time. Truckers also deserve our empathy when "F"s hinder the momentum of their big rigs. Contractors, electricians, plumbers . . . for many in the trades, their vehicles *are* their offices. Bus and limo drivers, tow truck and snowplow operators, and all others who drive for a living are entitled to extra consideration from the rest of us.

AMBULANCE

Let's kick things off with an "F"-isode where *everyone* should move aside—whenever an ambulance, fire truck, or police car is traveling with its lights flashing and sirens blaring. But "F"s sometimes put others at risk by failing to pull over.

So, "F"s, help me understand . . . the good people who are out there protecting us are in a hurry, following protocol by using their lights and sirens, and yet you make it difficult for them to do their jobs?

A little advice for you lunkheads: when you hear or see emergency vehicles, your *only* choice is to pull over to the right and stop.

Do *not*:

> Slam on your brakes and stop in the middle of a lane.
> Pull over to the left (that's the new trend according to my EMT friends).
> Gamble with everyone's safety by trying to reach your turn before you're caught.
> Pull in behind an emergency vehicle in an attempt to skirt through traffic.

It's in instances like these when you "F"s should picture one of *your* loved ones in that ambulance. (You do have loved ones, don't you?)

Due to the egregious nature of this particular offense, you'll notice that the "F" Meter is pegged at 100 percent jerk. Time for the **"F"-INATOR** to launch a message.

Here's the deal, "F"s . . . when you risk the lives of others, the **"F"-INATOR** *will* return the favor. ¿UNDERSTOOD?

I Want to Wring Your Rubberneck

Why do rubberneckers slow down when they see an accident? Do they do so to assist? No, they never leave their vehicles. For safety's sake? No, the accident is on the *other* side of the highway. Then why?

For some it's for the same reason they watch the evening news: they enjoy seeing others in distress.

For others it's because they literally have nothing better to do than gawk.

And for some it's poor coordination—when they look to the side they simply can't help but slow down.

And as we all know, rubberneckers find trouble wherever they go.

Far worse are jerks who rubberneck *without* slowing down. This next "F"-isode involved my nephew, who is an EMT and a card-carrying member of Class A if there ever was one.

He came across an accident in an HOV (High Occupancy Vehicle) lane on a highway's westbound side. My nephew was off duty and had been traveling eastbound. An SUV had flipped onto its roof, another car had major damage, and a man resting against a Jersey barrier was bleeding from the head.

The only professional to arrive on scene before my nephew was a state trooper, and he welcomed the support. The trooper instructed my nephew to engage his Jeep's emergency lights and to park in the median strip between the eastbound HOV lane and the primary traffic lanes.

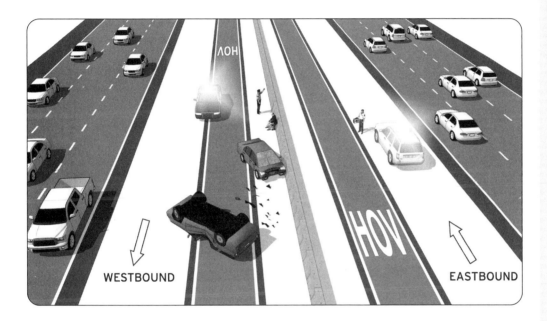

My nephew then crossed over to the westbound side to assess the injuries. An ambulance and fire truck arrived a few minutes later and the situation was brought under control.

You might think this was the end of the story, but no. Suddenly everyone heard a loud crash, a long screech, and a second loud crash . . . on the *eastbound* side.

That's right . . . a rubbernecking "F" traveling in the eastbound HOV lane had care-lessly veered to the right and slammed into my nephew's Jeep at 70 mph. His vehicle then spun sideways into the HOV lane only to be T-boned by yet *another* "F" who was also rubbernecking.

As incredible as this story sounds, I swear that it hasn't been embellished one bit.

It makes me want to burn rubber . . . rubber*necks*, that is.

Alice in Dunderland

Here's another classic case of in-"F"-titude. I was driving down the center lane of a six-lane divided highway when I spotted a state police cruiser in my rearview mirror. He was barreling down the left lane, apparently on a mission. As usual, a dunderheaded "F" was also in the left lane, plodding along as if his was the only vehicle on the road.

PROBLEM #1:

Like most "F"s, this twit was oblivious to his surroundings and therefore didn't notice the cruiser until the very last minute.

PROBLEM #2:

Once he finally did see the cruiser, his immediate solution was to slow down, thinking that he was somehow at risk.

Here's the deal, "F"s . . . if a police cruiser is traveling well above the speed limit without its warning lights flashing, then the officer's objective is elsewhere. The absolute last thing he needs is a twit like you in the left lane slowing him down. The proper course of action is to put on your turn signal and accelerate until you can move into a right-hand lane and let him go by.

This brings to mind the Queen of Hearts, the fictional monarch from *Alice in Wonderland*, who would scream, "Off with their heads!" as she decreed death sentences to her ("F") subjects. If only she were alive today . . .

Trivial Pursuit . . . *Not!*

Certainly there are people out there who commit crimes strictly out of desperation . . . inherently honest people who feel that crime is their only option due to the hand life has dealt them. But *all* crimes are committed by "F"s—either by "A"s gone bad or by "F"s who were simply born that way.

The reason television programs (reality and drama alike) about catching criminals are so immensely popular is that "A"s yearn to see justice prevail. We love it when "F"s are caught and punished. "F"s, on the other hand, probably watch these shows to cheer on their F-riends.

Police-chase videos are a mixed bag, though. While entertaining and exciting to watch, every chase puts other motorists, pedestrians, and police officers in harm's way.

ONE MISSTEP FOR "F"s . . . ONE GIANT LEAP FOR MANKIND!

If you're anything like me, you watch police-chase videos for only one reason: to see natural selection at work.

Eighteen-Wheeler Momentum Stealer

Most vehicles are able to maintain a constant speed when they hit an incline—a mild depression of the accelerator pedal is all it takes. Not so for large trucks. These rigs are designed to haul extremely heavy loads but not to accelerate quickly, and therefore any loss of momentum is a *huge* burden for them. "F"s manage to spread that burden onto the rest of us. Here's how:

When hitting an incline, some "F"s will drive so slowly that even an eighteen-wheeler is forced to move into the passing lane.

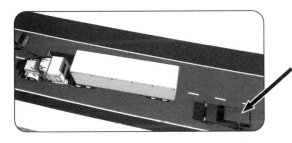

Invariably, another "F" will be driving well below the speed limit in the left lane, which gives the truck room to move over.

And finally, a third clueless "F" will match speed with the truck, preventing it from moving back into the right lane once it loses momentum.

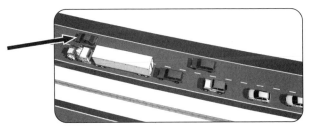

This trucker has done nothing fundamentally wrong, though the less observant among us would improperly target their frustrations toward him. But as usual, this problem was ultimately rooted in the behavior of ignorant "F"s.

And one last thing . . . I guarantee you that the third "F" in the above example will fail to follow the common practice of flashing his high beams even after it is safe for the trucker to pull back into the right lane. "F"s are nothing if not consistent.

⟨r⟩ In Case of Fire, Break Glass

This "F"-isode involved another nephew . . . a firefighter, paramedic, member of Class A, and brother of the EMT mentioned earlier in "I Want to Wring Your Rubberneck." There was a fire . . . and glass was broken.

My nephew's station responded to an alarm and arrived to find a fully-involved basement fire in a three-story dwelling. His chief instructed him to drop the attack hose and drive to the nearest hydrant. When he reached it, he found the hydrant completely blocked by an SUV that had been crammed in between two other vehicles.

By now his "brothers" were in the basement fighting a fire that involved a natural gas feed, and therefore they were rapidly consuming the water in the truck's tank. My nephew knew that time was of the essence, so he made what was, to me and many others, the logical choice—go *through* the SUV. He knocked out both rear windows, dragged the hose through the inside of the vehicle, and attached it to the hydrant. Problem solved.

When asked to justify his actions, my nephew cited the obvious physical limitations of the scene, but he mainly felt that "F"s like this needed to be taught a lesson. By blocking a hydrant, the SUV driver had "made a statement" that his needs were more important than the lives and property of others. Perhaps my nephew did not take the path of least resistance, but it was certainly the most instructive.

When the vehicle owner finally returned, he foolishly admitted that "he'd parked there for years and it had never mattered before!" That explanation earned him a tasty stack of tickets from the police and fire departments for an array of violations.

"F" sprinting back to the scene of the crime...

The incident received local and national news coverage, as the message was heard loud and clear—*don't* block a fire hydrant. My nephew reported that later in the week and for months thereafter, his department didn't notice a single vehicle parked even remotely close to a hydrant.

Final Score:

Firemen: 1	"F"s: 0

Not So Special Delivery

Picture the endless joy one must experience as an express delivery driver forced to contend with "F"s as part and parcel (pun intended) of the daily job. That would be like an "F" shutting down your computer every time you left your office for a moment or hiding your hand tools whenever you went to the stockroom for supplies.

We've all experienced scenes like the one displayed below. This time a delivery truck was prevented from taking a right turn on red because an idiot in front of him didn't move into the *wide open* left lane.

At a red light, an "F" who was *not* turning right blocked the right lane...

...even though this lane was wide open.

For most it would be a mere annoyance, but for delivery drivers it could quite possibly mean the inability to complete their routes on time.

"F"s will defend themselves by saying that they are not breaking any law by sitting in the right lane. I suppose that's true . . . by blocking others in this manner, "F"s *legally* demonstrate a complete lack of courtesy.

Time once again to call upon the **"F"-INATOR** to demonstrate its high degree of "magnetism."

Wouldn't the world be a better place if "F"s were dragged aside whenever they dragged their feet?

Uneasy Riders

There is one last Class-A subgroup that, in my humble opinion, deserves the moniker of "road warriors"—those who ride motorcycles. Unlike most of us, who are enveloped within our vehicles, a biker's only protection is usually limited to his own coordination and a helmet. While this book's "F"-isodes demonstrate how most "A"s become merely frustrated by "F"s, those same bonehead maneuvers can routinely be matters of life and death to a biker.

I fully understand that riding vs. driving is a choice—bikers don't *have* to ride (although some would argue that point)—but a biker has every right to make that choice, just as you may choose to drive a Mini instead of a Hummer. And with rising gas prices, the decision to ride could be based on economics . . . it was for me when I owned a motorcycle in college.

With bikers as with everything else, there are an annoying minority who give the majority a bad name. Those with excessively loud mufflers are a good example, for the noise serves no real purpose other than to satisfy their insecure owners' need for attention.

Or those who weave through heavy traffic as shown here.

But most bikers are careful, attentive, and considerate.

Here are a few road rules to follow. We can easily show a little extra consideration without being terribly inconvenienced:

(1) Let motorcycles proceed between lanes in stop-and-go traffic. It's one of the few times when bikers have the advantage, so let them be. Call it payback for all those times they've had to huddle beneath overpasses during a rainstorm as we drove comfortably by.

(2) Don't be offended when bikers leave their high beams on. It's an intentional safety measure—their best way to ensure that you see them.

(3) Understand why bikers ride toward the center line and not in the middle of their lane. It's not to intimidate or annoy you. Instead they do this for two reasons:

(a) Oil accumulates as it drips from passing vehicles, making the middle of many lanes slippery and dangerous for motorcycles.

(b) Moving toward the center line is the safer option because unexpected obstacles (dogs, for instance) are more apt to appear from the roadside.

Bikers tend to have bad reputations—very few deserve it.

EXIT 10

Truck Me All to Hell

'm close, personal friends with many long-haul truckers. Most are extremely steady drivers who are very safety conscious. But as we've seen before, every population has its bad seeds—some are careless, and others are intentionally annoying. We'll expose both.

Let's begin by examining why large trucks evoke irrational fear in the minds of so many "F"s.

Tear Off the Band-Aid®, N-i-c-e and S-l-o-w

I'd like to ask you "F"s to explain your (lack of) reasoning when traveling in the left lane and about to pass an eighteen-wheeler.

As you approach the truck, you decelerate.

When you finally muster the courage to drive past the truck, you slow down even *more*.

As a result, traffic backs up as this scene plays out.

Now, anyone with half a brain would realize that most truckers are better drivers than the rest of us . . . you know, *because they do it for a living*. Therefore, there's little risk that they'll suddenly dart into your lane and crush you.

Be that as it may, I would think that if you were afraid to pass a truck, you'd want to do it as *quickly* as possible . . . right? (That's a rhetorical question . . . of course I'm right—I'm in Class A.) You don't slowly tear off a Band-Aid® that's stuck to the hair on your arm, do you? No, you rip it off to get it over with. Then why do you creep past eighteen-wheelers which evoke in you such fear?

The strangest part is that once you've finally made it into the open, you speed up again, rejoicing like a trapped animal that's just been released. In this case, however, you built your own trap in the first place.

I'll need more than a Band-Aid® to relieve the headache you've given me.

Did You Just Cut One?

This "F"-isode reviews a classic "brain fart," not limited to truckers, but certainly more prevalent with them.

I was traveling down the left lane of a four-lane divided highway. Up ahead was an eighteen-wheeler following a few cars in the right lane. As I approached the group, I felt my anticipation build as I envisioned what was about to happen.

Here I come...

As usual, the truck stayed in the right lane until the *very* last minute, at which point he veered into the left lane to cut me off.

There was no one behind me, so the trucker could have waited two seconds, but no . . . over he came.

Okay . . . a few things to note. First of all, after the trucking "F" entered the left lane, he didn't immediately pass the cars that were traveling in the right lane. This reinforced what I already knew—that he was in fact previously going the same speed as those cars and only pulled into the left lane to be an ass.

WHO KNEW?
...actually, I did...

"F" takes his sweet time making the pass.

Then, after what felt like an hour, he had finally passed the three cars. Of course, he *stayed* in the left lane. I gave this a nanosecond, pulled into the right lane, and reengaged my cruise control.

Most "F"s would have cut me off again as soon as they saw me pull to the right, but this one sped up instead. How did I know this?

(a) I can judge speed.

(b) His engine began to wail as I passed him.

And no, it didn't end there. After a short time I caught up with more vehicles in the right lane, prompting me to pull back into the left lane to pass them.

I was at *least* one hundred feet ahead of the "F" when I did this, but he flashed his lights at me anyway.

It was comical . . . the halfwit's high beams merely confirmed that his actions had been intentional all along.

Large vehicle . . . small mind.

 **Spatter Up!**

It's frustrating when truckers can't manage to keep all eighteen wheels on the main road. These particular twits drift onto warning strips and shoulders, invariably spraying debris all over other, smaller vehicles.

Then there are those overloaded construction trucks that spew dirt and gravel onto our vehicles when they hit bumps in the road. Nice.

Last are the trucks with loose junk in their beds. I once saw a three-car accident caused by wind lifting a loose piece of paneling from a pickup truck's bed.

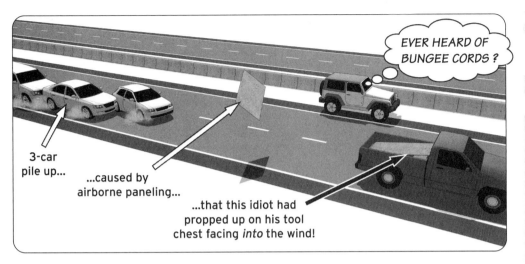

3-car pile up...

...caused by airborne paneling...

...that this idiot had propped up on his tool chest facing *into* the wind!

EVER HEARD OF BUNGEE CORDS ?

My best solution to these issues is the imposition of massive fines when they occur.

Or . . . a visit from the **"F"-INATOR**.

IT'S HAMMER TIME !

Stranded in the Middle of Nowhere

Generally speaking, truckers are unfairly criticized. When a trucker *appears* to be driving aggressively, far more often than not an "F" has pushed him into that situation. A classic example is shown here.

At first glance, the unobservant among us would accuse the white truck of aggressive driving, but this "F"-isode's true culprit is the idiot in front of him.

On most six-lane divided highways, trucks are prohibited from using the left lane. So in this situation, the white truck is essentially stranded—the right lane is blocked, and he can't legally enter the left lane. Therefore, the "F" in front of him should either move into the open left lane or accelerate so he can move to the right . . . anything but loafing along in the middle lane.

Since almost every product we use today is delivered to us by truck, we should go out of our way to help truckers do their jobs.

EXIT 11

Cops & Robbers

Before taking this EXIT, I would like to reaffirm my respect for the police. If it weren't for them, our society would crumble. End of story. They take on the tough jobs that the rest of us aren't willing to tackle, dealing with the dregs of society and putting themselves in harm's way to keep us safe. Firefighters are cut from the same cloth. So are all of those whose primary job function is caring for others.

But cops become robbers when they engage in one specific activity—speed traps. Through them, in one form or another, our time and money are virtually stolen from us. This EXIT includes several classic examples.

You'll also be introduced to the Keystone Cops and "F" Troop, imposters who ineffectively imitate the functions of legitimate police officers. In this EXIT's last "F"–isode, I'll share with you a "conversation" I once had with one of these traffic cops for hire.

⚡ Foot Traffic

Okay, "F"s, explain this one to me:

A cop has someone pulled over for speeding . . .

. . . he's standing *next* to that vehicle writing out a ticket . . .

. . . yet you slow down anyway.

What's he going to do, chase you down on foot?

Worst of all, you "F"s usually drop to well *below* the speed limit when you see a cop. Come on already!

The only slack I'll cut anyone, as I alluded to earlier, is that speed traps are over-used. I wouldn't mind so much if tickets were handed out for speeders *and* impeders, because after all, "F"s who drive under the speed limit trigger more problems than those of us who drive slightly over it.

Look, I accept that idiots who drive recklessly deserve to be ticketed. But let me ask my fellow "A"s a question: how many of you have ever received a speeding ticket? I suspect that many of you have. Now, how many of you are reckless drivers? *Very* few of you, I'm sure.

There it is in a nutshell—most speeding tickets are handed out to good people who do not drive recklessly. Meanwhile, the dopes who plod along in everyone's way are left completely alone. Not fair . . . not right.

Speedy Guns Alice

Speedy Gonzales: the "fastest mouse in all Mexico."
Speedy Guns Alice: a wimp with a hyper-aversion to speed guns.

It's bad enough that "F"s slow down for speed traps even when they're not speeding, but can anyone explain why they also slow down for speed traps located on the *other* side of the highway?

A speed trap on the other side... ...causes "Alice" to brake on *this* side!

The last time I checked, police cars weren't equipped to traverse guardrails and Jersey barriers. Can "F"s be any less intelligent? (Actually, we're only about two-thirds of the way through the book, so let's reserve judgment on that for now.)

In a related example, on my way home from work one evening, traffic was backed up on the highway for about half a mile. As I slowly rounded a bend, the reason for the backup became apparent ... another set of flashing blue lights.

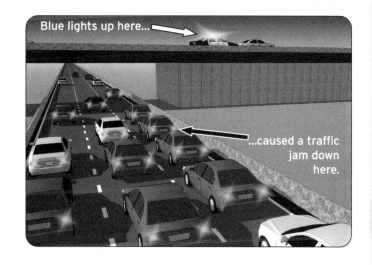

Blue lights up here... ...caused a traffic jam down here.

But *this* time the cop in question had someone pulled over on a cross road.

Thaaaat's right ... "F"s on the interstate were slowing down because they saw police lights on an *overpass*.

Un ... be ... *lievable!*

I Wish You Would Shut Your Trap

This "F"-isode presents a caricature of speed traps if there ever was one.

There's a highway exit ramp in my county that slopes significantly downward to a two-lane service road. The ramp morphs into a third lane at this juncture. The area is strictly commercial.

Here's the rub: the service road's speed limit is 25 mph.

No, that's not a misprint! After exiting a 65-mph interstate highway onto a downward-sloping exit ramp leading to what becomes a three-lane service road in a *non*-residential area, some genius decided that the speed limit should be 25 mph. And, by the way, the speed limit sign is on the far *right* side of the service road, across the three-lane road from the ramp.

This happened to be my exit on the way to play golf one morning. I was in no particular hurry and there was virtually no traffic on the service road. I coasted down the ramp, my foot not once having touched the accelerator pedal since I'd left the highway. Barely after I merged with the service road, I rounded a slight bend and came upon two motorcycle cops. Like another sap before me, I was bagged— "51 in a 25"—for $260. Let me ask you . . . isn't it usually robbers who stalk you from the woods and then jump out and point a gun at you?

While another hard-working member of Class A is about to be clipped for $260...

...I envision a drug deal going down unnoticed on the other side of this fence.

Now, we all know the drill. Once pulled over, we're typically made to wait an inordinate amount of time as an officer fills in what amounts to ten boxes on a standard form (I've seen that take as long as fifteen minutes). But not *that* morning—I had my ticket and was back on the road in less than a minute (after some obligatory disdain thrown my way by the officer—"You really *must* slow down," he blurted).

Does anyone want to guess what day of the month it was? Yes, that's right . . . it was the *last* day, July 31. Can you say, "Revenue quota"? What a valuable use of police officers' time!

They don't call them traps for nothing.

 **Keystone Cops**

What's wrong with this picture?

Traffic is flowing along smoothly from the left, but it's all jammed up from the other direction. Let's zoom in and take a closer look.

"F" !

HEY ! I'M GONNA CRACK OPEN MY LUNCH. WANT HALF MY SANDWICH ?

HOW ABOUT YOU WAIT UNTIL THERE'S NO TRAFFIC ?!

Ah, yes. Please tell me that none of you were surprised to find that this mess was rooted in the behavior of a clueless "F".

Instead of hiring a qualified police officer to control this scene, I guarantee you that some bureaucrat decided he could save a little money by using a traffic cop for hire. These "Keystone Cops" are almost always more interested in their next coffee break or their next cell phone call than the job at hand.

Sometimes "F"s-for-hire add insult to injury by adopting a warped sense of self-importance. There's a name for "F"s like those . . . see the next page.

 "F" Troop

As discussed in the prior "F"-isode, imposters are often hired in lieu of real police officers. These imposters are reminiscent of Corporal Agarn from the classic television show, *F Troop*.

Many of them adopt a power-broker mentality—the same one displayed by many "F"'s who work at motor vehicle departments. They become large and in charge, expecting you to accept your position *well* down in the pecking order. One time you'll see such a power broker surface is when they're directing traffic. (Have you *ever* seen an intersection flow more smoothly with a traffic cop involved? No, I didn't think so.)

Here's a real-life example: I pulled into a furniture store parking lot one Sunday morning and found an "F" Trooper "helping" customers park. (I'm pretty sure that I could have found a space on my own, but whatever.)

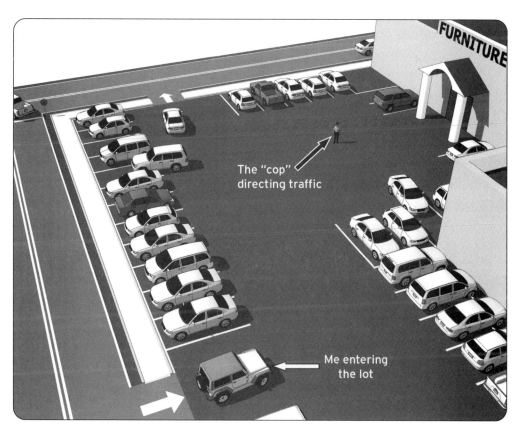

As I entered the lot, he gave me the typical "talk to the hand" gesture, so I dutifully stopped.

Minivan backing out

After a moment he waved me on, but just as he did a minivan in my path started to back out. So I waited. This prompted the "F" to wave more and more vigorously (he hadn't noticed the mini-van). I continued waiting so the minivan didn't back into me.

The "F" then began shaking his head in disgust. He thought I was waiting for a spot closer to the store entrance, evidenced by him shouting to me, "Go ahead, you can have *that* spot," as I finally rolled in his direction.

I'll admit that by now I had him squarely pegged as a round "hole," so the following conversation ensued as I inched past him:

Me: "Were you shaking your head at *me*?"

Him: "Yes. I waved you on but you didn't move."

Me: "I didn't ask why."

Him: "What?"

Me: "I only asked *if* you were shaking your head at me, not *why*."

Him: Silence.

Me: "Didn't see the minivan right away, did you?"

Him: (after a telltale pause) "I saw it!"

Me: "Uh huh. You have a real special day now, okay?"

I kept going and parked, and as I exited my car, I was surprised to find him confronting me, actually bumping me with his chest as I closed my car door!

Because his short fuse was equaled by his short stature, a vision of Yosemite Sam suddenly popped into my head.

Sam: "Got anything else to say, tough guy?"

Me: "Yes. Touch me again and I'll press charges."

Sam: "One more word and I'll have you downtown in front of a judge."

Me: "That would be an *excellent* place for me to press charges."

Sam: "Get out of my sight . . . you dagnabit rabbit!"

Okay . . . so I made up that last part. But he did actually come up with, "Get out of my sight" all on his own . . . wasn't that clever?

I shouldn't have contributed to this confrontation, but when "Sam" decided to unjustly ruin my day (in this case a *Sun*day), I wasn't in the mood to turn the other cheek. No, it was an eye for an eye this time . . . even though this clown couldn't quite *look* me in the eye.

EXIT 12

You Take Your Toll on Me

There are far too many toll roads in this country. Toll booths are expensive to build, they cost additional taxpayer money to staff, they create congestion and cause accidents, they waste the time of every person driving through them, and maybe worst of all, every vehicle idling in line harms our environment. We should definitely be able to find more efficient ways to tax and fund highway construction projects than via these leftover relics of a bygone era.

And you'd think that navigating through toll booths would be pretty straightforward, right? Yet routinely I witness the misuse of cars-only lanes, confusion over the function of transponders in automated toll lanes, and irrational moves that create congestion where there should be none. The fact that so much absurdity can surround a simple act of paying a toll remains a mystery to me.

This EXIT also addresses the disconnect between ongoing toll collections and the poor condition of our roads and transportation infrastructure.

A Point to "Ponder"

Many toll booths now feature "EZ Pass" or "Fast Lane" systems, which recognize vehicle transponders as they pass through at a certain speed. This is a wonderful, time-saving invention. But more often than not I'll end up behind a moron who stops and waits for a green light before proceeding through the toll booth. This temporarily turns "my" Fast Lane into a plain, old, stop-and-go toll lane.

An "F" sees the "15 mph" sign, and it prompts him to appropriately slow down . . .

. . . then he comes to a *complete* stop because none of the lights on the pole are lit . . .

... and only *after* the light turns green does he start moving again.

Yo, "F"s—the 15-mph speed limit sign on Fast Lanes indicates that you can actually keep moving. In case you haven't noticed, these lanes include cameras that are there not only to catch people going through the tolls without paying but also to ensure proper billing if your transponder or the lane's detection device malfunctions. In other words, even if the light doesn't turn green *you can still proceed.*

And by the way, this is one place where the old speed *limit* signs should still apply. Too many toll collectors have been killed or injured by reckless jerks who fly through express lanes at far too great a speed!

(Trans)ponder that . . .

All Dogs Are Mammals, but Not All Mammals Are Dogs

People in Class A recognize this "F"-isode's title as a statement of Boolean logic, which is the language of "if-thens," "ands," "ors," and "buts." Boolean logic is the basis of mathematics, computer science, philosophy, and law. A real-world (mis)application of this logic is shown below, which is further proof that "F"s never spent enough time on their schoolwork.

Here's what tends to happen:

> "F"s pull up to a toll booth and see the "cars only" sign.
> They're in a *car*, so they automatically pull into the lane that's designated as *only* for cars.
> A backup forms in that lane, causing other lanes to be clear (which, for once, helps us "A"s).

Hey, "F"s . . ."cars only" doesn't mean cars are *required* to use that lane—it means that only cars are *allowed* to.

But now that I think about it, I hope that you "F"s will ignore this lesson since it's one of the few times that your limited IQs actually save me time.

What's with the Swerve, Merv?

Another strange phenomenon is rogue truckers who are unable (or refuse) to steer their rigs properly as they exit a toll booth. This may stem from carelessness or lack of ability, but usually I believe it's intentional (it's too stupid to be otherwise).

Sometimes when I exit a toll booth behind an eighteen-wheeler, he'll swing wide in the opposite direction of the one in which he's ultimately headed. Why, you ask? The need to impede—what else?

I personally know and respect many truckers. Most are competent, considerate drivers. But as I've noted before, every population segment has its bad seeds. These particular halfwits apparently see nothing wrong with impeding as many people as possible with their rigs. Instead of focusing on the job (which, as you know by now, "F"s don't do), they seem hell-bent on aggravating others.

You really know how to strike a nerve, Merv.

Choosing Sides

The PROBLEM:

Massive congestion on this side of the toll booth, whereas the other side is wide open.

The CAUSE:

"F"s erroneously believing that they must move into their intended lane *before* they go through the toll booth.

A quick look at the illustration below tells it all. It only takes a few dopes forcing their way across the lanes leading *into* a toll booth for an entire commute to be ruined.

The better approach is to wait until *after* you've gone through a toll booth to change lanes. "F"s, do you know why that is? (Of course you don't . . . so read on.)

The vast majority of the time, as illustrated on the prior page, toll booths will be more congested on the approach than on the departure. The reason for this is very simple: at any given time there will be virtually the same number of vehicles entering a toll plaza as leaving it, but those entering are *de*celerating while those leaving are *ac*celerating. Accelerating vehicles disperse more quickly, therefore it's smarter to cross into your lane *after* you've exited the tolls.

This is another time when I can only imagine what goes on in the minds of "F"s:

> ❯ Some of it must be sheer ignorance . . . they feel that they're actually doing the polite thing by moving into the correct lane before paying their toll.

> ❯ Some could be due to a lack of coordination . . . since "F"s didn't play sports as children and therefore never developed hand-eye coordination or proper spatial perception, they're only capable of merging through slow-moving, stop-and-go traffic.

> ❯ Some are out of touch with reality . . . they must visualize a solid wall that would physically prevent them from changing lanes if they waited until after exiting the toll booth.

> ❯ Most are simply morons.

All of this makes my head (and sides) hurt. Is it just me?

Shake, Rattle & Roll

Entire books have been written about America's crumbling infrastructure. I'll give it a page here, since other books in my Why It's Your Fault™ series will explore this topic in greater depth.

Many of us pay tolls on a regular basis, but each time our vehicles shake and rattle as we roll over a pothole, we wonder where all that toll money goes. The condition of our roads, bridges, and tunnels is worsening by the day, costing us time and money while also jeopardizing our safety.

I say it's time we replaced our elected "F"-icials with representatives from Class A who will spend our tax dollars on "*U.S.*" . . . that's right, the United States . . . so we can get back to the days when driving throughout this wonderful country of ours was far more enjoyable.

EXIT 13

Tailgating
and
Football

*T*his EXIT explores my favorite examples of "grid-irony." Sometimes "F"s drive so slowly that they deserve to be tailgated. (That doesn't mean you should do it, however . . . it just means that they deserve it.) "A"s, on the other hand, should *never* be tailgated. Why? Because we will, by definition, travel at the safe, correct speed unless we're behind a lumbering "F". End of discussion.

Here's a visual to help "F"s understand this issue.

If you can read this, you're an "F"!

⬦ The Incomplete P(ass)

Hey, "F", if for some reason you pull up behind me . . .

. . . and I politely move aside . . .

. . . then would you please *go by me* already?

When you don't go by, you're guilty of an "incomplete pass." To avoid being boxed in, don't be surprised if I accelerate, pull *back* into the your lane, and reset my cruise control at whatever speed I choose.

(A question for my Class-A friends: would I be penalized for "roughing the passer" if I were to shove an "F" like this into a guardrail? Of course I would. That's why I dreamed up the **"F"-INATOR** . . .)

◇ Unsportsmanlike Conduct

Hey, "F"s . . . when you pass me on the left, what itch do you scratch by immediately pulling back into my lane? All this does is force me to involuntarily tailgate.

Our safety is further compromised when you do this in unfavorable weather, not to mention all the crap you kick up onto my car. Very unsportsmanlike!

Look, if you're too emasculate to remain in the left lane until it's safe to pull back to the right, you should stop using that lane in the first place, loser.

⟨Y⟩ Delay of Game

Answer this next one, "F". We're on a six-lane divided highway, traffic is light, I'm in the middle lane with my cruise control set to 75 mph, and you pull up from behind and tailgate me.

This goes on for miles. Instead of passing me, you continue to ride my tail in the middle lane.

So just for fun I pull into the right lane to test what will happen. But there's no mystery. With 100-percent certainty—it's happened *every* time I've done this—you'll speed up and pass me.

This means that for all of those tailgating miles *my* speed dictated *your* speed, right?

Caught in your own little "delay of game" there, weren't you?

P(ass) Interference

Here's another case where "F"'s force us to tailgate.

I'll be traveling in the left lane in heavy traffic, maintaining a safe following distance, when an "F" will squeeze his way into the gap between me and the vehicle just ahead. As a result, the "F" and I are now both following too closely.

This will usually happen when there's a much larger gap behind me, but instead of waiting for a brief moment to let me go by, the "F" selfishly stuffs himself into my lane.

This would be definitely be classified as offensive pass interference.

EXIT 14

Roadpourri

Potpourri: a collection of miscellaneous literary extracts.

Roadpourri: a collection of miscellaneous road rage "F"-isodes.

This EXIT explores the plague of backseat drivers, reviews various gas station indiscretions, lambastes polluters over their lack of etiquette, teaches us how to take the bull**** by the horn, and introduces new characters, such as the little-known eighth dwarf—Lazy.

Backseat Drivers

This "F"-isode's title is a common misnomer since the useless ramblings of back-seat drivers typically emanate from the seat immediately to our right. The sad irony is that the very same "F"s who accuse us of having road rage are responsible for fueling those emotions with their incessant blabbering. Here are some of my favorites . . . if you can call them that.

A final word to the "F"s—always remember that your opinions should take a "backseat" to ours.

✛ Pain in the Gas

My first "gas pain" stems from full-serve-only stations. I avoid them like the plague because so many are staffed with mental dropouts who can't manage to remove a nozzle without spilling gas onto my car.

One time this occurred when I had borrowed my dad's car, and I had to use the station's windshield fluid and squeegee to clean up the mess. Believe it or not, the attendant "F" actually complained! (As you might have imagined, I completely ignored him.)

I also feel gas pain when I'm behind a twit who stops at the *first* open pump instead of politely pulling as far ahead as possible. Very considerate, "F".

Oh, and let's not forget those jerks who, after they've finished pumping, leave their vehicles at the pump while they go inside to shop. It's "all about me" taken to a whole new level.

Another flagrant violation of gas-station etiquette occurred in my presence recently, and the sequence of events made me believe, if only for a fleeting moment, that everything was suddenly right with the world.

This particular gas station was laid out to facilitate all vehicles flowing through in the same direction. I was at the second pump when a pickup truck at the first pump in front of me finished and pulled away.

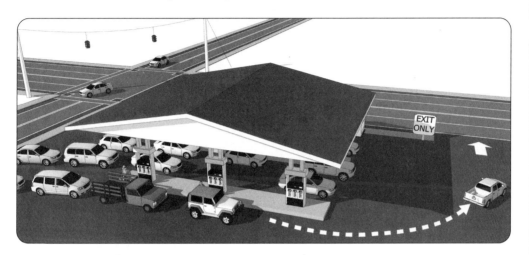

Then an "F" pulled in from the wrong side, brought his car nose to nose with mine, and got out. I looked at him and shook my head in disgust. He forced an unconvincing "What are you looking at?" stare, which I didn't acknowledge.

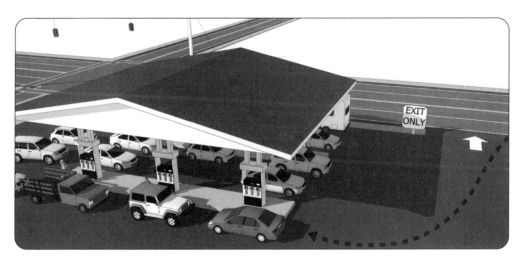

You certainly know by now that I'm not an advocate of initiating confrontations, but the guy at the pump behind me sure was. I heard a door close and turned to see "Large Lewis" walking away from his construction truck and past me with a hammer in his hand.

I'll admit that I couldn't decide whether I wanted Large to use his hammer on the car or the "F" himself, but I knew I'd be happy either way.

Instead, he walked up to the "F" and said something in a voice so quiet that I couldn't make it out from a mere ten feet away.

As a result, the "F" immediately did a 180-degree turn, just about dove back into his car, and sped away. Mr. Lewis smiled on his way by and said . . .

Classic!

 ## No Smoking

What should we do with "F"s who refuse to maintain their vehicle engines in proper working order? Or what about those who intentionally perpetuate the problem by cheating their way through annual state inspections?

Since these "F"s seem intent on contributing to global warming, maybe we should issue them a global *warning*—that the **"F"-INATOR** is headed their way.

Courtesy Is No Longer Common

Although experience suggests that I do otherwise, I still sometimes allow pedestrians to cross my path—at an intersection, a crosswalk—wherever. Would you like to know what happens all too often? Yes, they *saunter* across and don't wave to thank me.

Once upon a time, people would run or at least jog across, smiling and waving back as a "thank you" for such a kind gesture. Not in *this* day and age, however. It's no wonder people become less and less friendly, less and less courteous . . . because courtesy is so rarely acknowledged. Even we "A"s become worn down and feed into to the decline of society as we become less polite ourselves.

The same thing happens when you hold doors open for people. No longer do they step up their pace in order to not keep *you* waiting. No "thank you," no smiles, and rarely even any eye contact. "F"s act as if they're somehow *entitled* to this action on our part . . . *"Yes, after you, your majesty."* Give me a break! Most "F"s won't even return a hello or salutation. There was a time when it would have been unconscionable to not at least return a greeting. No longer, it seems.

The morals that once made this a great country are vanishing before our eyes, as evidenced by these tiny, thoughtless acts. The mentality that drives this rude behavior is pervasive in *everything* "F"s do . . . on *and* off the road.

When It Rains . . . Up Yours!

How hard is it to avoid splashing pedestrians? The answer: *not* very.

Let me break it down into easy steps for you "F"s:

(a) It's raining.

(b) There are likely to be puddles.

(c) You see pedestrians.

(d) Therefore, you should either slow down or steer around the puddles.

Cops should hand out *huge* fines for this egregious behavior since it does nothing but waste people's time, money, and heartbeats.

Time for the **"F"-INATOR** to flush out the problem . . .

. . . while an old song plays in the background:

> I'm plunging in the rain
> Just plunging in the rain
> What a glorious feelin'
> I'm happy again . . .

Nervous Breakdown

There are two scenarios where "F"s give me a nervous breakdown.

The first covers "F"s who speed along breakdown lanes during traffic jams as others wait patiently. This puts everyone at risk because speeding vehicles are passing so closely to those which are barely moving. And this maneuver could also ultimately clog the breakdown lane and make it impossible for emergency vehicles to pass if necessary.

THAT'S THE BREAKDOWN LANE, "F"!

I do *not* advocate trying to block "F"s from doing this because such an action only increases the risk that an emergency vehicle will be unable to use the breakdown lane in a crisis. Unfortunately, this is one time when we need to let "F"s be "F"s. All we can do is give them the cold shoulder.

For short distances (no more than one-tenth of a mile) and at very low speeds (25 mph or less), using a breakdown lane is acceptable for vehicles *exiting* a highway. When used with caution, this strategy actually helps to relieve congestion.

My second nervous breakdown involves "F"s who stop wherever their tires go flat and immediately commence changing them.

On a highway I once saw an "F" milling around his driver's side as if he were in his own driveway, oblivious to the traffic whipping by him less than two feet away.

In another instance, not three hundred yards past the location of such an impromptu and ill-advised pit stop the shoulder widened considerably, providing what would have been a much safer area for an "F" to effect repairs.

On yet another occasion, an "F" stopped to change a flat tire at the very beginning of an exit ramp. Had he been born with even a trace of sensory neurons, he would have used the ramp to remove himself from danger.

Relatively speaking, vehicle rims are inexpensive. It's usually worth the potential cost of replacing a rim if it allows you to move to a safe location. If your vehicle is *completely* disabled, call 911 and request that an emergency vehicle either tow you to safety or provide warning lights while you make repairs. Anything but pulling these ridiculous and dangerous moves.

Fast Food for Slow People

Far too often I've found myself behind an "F" in a drive-thru as they proceeded to order for "fifty people."

There are so many things wrong with that:

> No planning—they could have called ahead (even fast food joints will pull an order in advance if asked to).

> Laziness—when ordering for so many people, they could get a little exercise for once by walking inside.

> Lack of consideration—good people use drive-thrus to save time, not to sit behind inconsiderate twerps.

Then they extend their time-wasting antics by checking their order *before* pulling away from the window, frequently finding something wrong with it . . . or so they think.

It looks like the **"F"-INATOR** is getting pretty "fed up" . . .

Hey "F", when slow people like you order fast food, isn't that an oxy, moron?

Steer Clear

Pop quiz: what's the best way to avoid most accidents?

a) Slam on the brakes, steer straight ahead, and hope for the best.

b) Steer around it.

c) Stay home.

Okay, I admit, it's a trick question. "F"s will instinctively slam on the brakes while plowing straight ahead, so *their* best option in avoiding an accident is c) Stay home.

But "A"s possess proper instincts and therefore realize that steering will prevent *far* more accidents than braking. The correct answer for us is b) Steer around it.

Statistically, the average car takes approximately 175 feet to come to a complete stop from 70 mph. If there's trouble immediately ahead, you've got about sixty yards to work with. If you use *only* your brakes, this is often not sufficient. See illustration **(1)**.

Conversely, a quick flick of the steering wheel will put you to the *side* of most trouble in less than twenty-five feet (and that's assuming you steer only 15 degrees off center). Even if you don't react immediately, in a mere fifty feet you can easily clear most trouble by steering to the side. See illustration **(2)**.

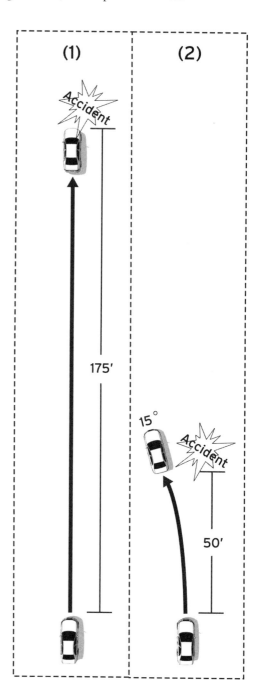

During the course of writing this book, I witnessed the following "F"-isode. On a busy, four-lane divided (but not limited-access) highway, a minivan darted from a parking lot into the path of oncoming traffic. An "F" ahead of me slammed on his brakes and skidded straight into the minivan. I steered into the left lane and dodged the collision . . . I would have hit them both had I not.

By the way . . . I already *knew* the left lane was clear because:

(a) I pay attention,

(b) I anticipate, and

(c) I try to avoid traveling with a vehicle in the adjacent lane.

In other words, I'm in Class A.

The irrefutable conclusion: most accidents will be more effectively prevented by using your steering wheel instead of just your brakes.

Are we clear . . . on how to steer?

Your Taste in Music Doesn't Interest Me

We've all heard vehicles driving by with music blaring at an excessive volume level. In fact, sometimes you can hear the music clearly even when the culprit's windows aren't open. This music also tends to be especially heavy on the bass, making it that much more annoying.

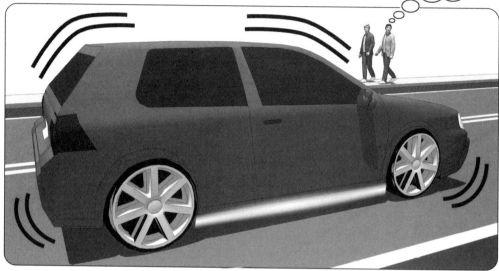

Hey, "F"s, if you want to make yourselves go deaf, that's your prerogative. (Prerogative means "right," by the way . . . no, not as in left vs. right . . . it means . . . oh, forget it!)

And you've already been told that we in Class A don't care what you think, right? Well guess what? We couldn't care less what type of music you listen to either.

The same thing applies to those of you with "malfunctioning" mufflers, whether they are on a car or a motorcycle. It's obvious that loud music and tailpipes are your way of compensating for other inadequacies.

Are you hearing me?

If not, maybe you'd like to hear from the **"F"-INATOR**?

A Different Kind of Moving Violation

As I followed an "F" down a back road the other day, we came across a moving van parked on the roadside. It was taking up most of our lane, and the road bent slightly to the right just past the van.

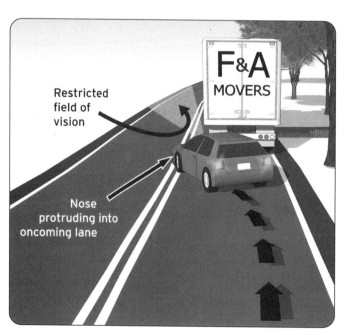

Restricted field of vision

Nose protruding into oncoming lane

The "F" continued to drive down our lane until he was immediately behind the moving van, and only *then* did he steer left to try and see around it. The angle he'd created for himself required him to stick the nose of his car into the oncoming lane in order for his field of vision to clear the van. And even then it was restricted.

Me, on the other hand? I hugged the center line so I could see well past the van and down the street. In this case no traffic was coming (I had to wait "patiently" for the "F" to figure that out). If there had been traffic, they still would have had sufficient room on their side of the road, even with me hugging the center line.

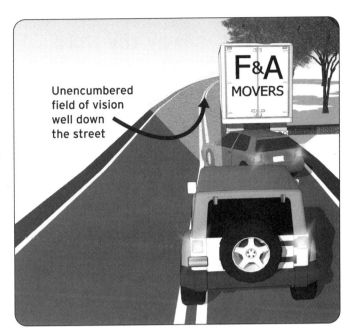

Unencumbered field of vision well down the street

Just another case of when "F"s should either improve or move (preferably to another galaxy).

Bull**** by the Horn

"A"s use a little thing called anticipation to avoid problematic situations. When problems are unavoidable, we react first with our steering wheels and brakes and only use our horns as a last resort.

"F"s, though, drive along blindly, "instinctively" beeping their horns the moment they're surprised. Let's think about it and try to come up with even one instance where laying on a horn ever changed anything for the better. No? I didn't think so. A quick beep always does the job.

An extended horn blast (which is the vehicular equivalent of giving someone the finger) merely confirms that a driver is an inattentive dweeb, someone unable to anticipate the trouble that now compels him to be heard. Idiots like these are routinely oblivious to the fact that they painted themselves into the proverbial corner in the first place.

I saw an example of this the other day as someone tried to merge onto a highway from an entrance ramp. An "F" who was already on the highway saw this person merging, but instead of politely moving into the left lane (which was totally clear), the "F" chose to lay on his horn instead.

Wise choice, idiot.

I suggest that vehicle manufacturers be required to modify the way horns function. No matter how long you hold them down, horns should be set to beep briefly and then stop.

A little hint: you know you're an "F" if your horn stays on long enough to create the Doppler effect.

If you don't know what that *is*, **then look it up, moron** . . .

Dopey, Sleepy, and the Eighth Dwarf—Lazy

I've only seen three of the famous seven . . . make that eight . . . dwarves behind the wheel:

Dopey: an "F" driving drunk or otherwise impaired.

Sleepy: a pinhead who falls asleep at the wheel.

Lazy: any "F" who litters.

Let's start with Dopey. I would never assert that all alcoholics are a threat to our public safety. Most keep their disease in check and don't drink and drive. Those that do? They're "F"s. The same goes for sh*t-faced party-goers who binge-drink or do drugs before taking the wheel. It's a travesty when people are killed or injured by these "F"s. (On the other hand, when "F"s kill *themselves* in this manner . . . isn't that just Darwinism at its finest?)

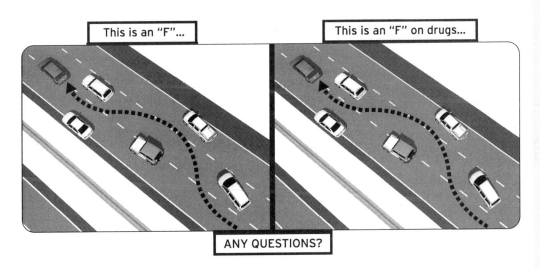

This is an "F"...

This is an "F" on drugs...

ANY QUESTIONS?

And "F"s who fall asleep at the wheel (a.k.a. Sleepy) are equally accountable. I guarantee you that not one person in a million has a justifiable reason for driving while overtired. Highway signs are right on target when they remind us to, "Take a break . . . stay awake . . . for safety's sake."

Last, let's meet Lazy. What compels an "F" to litter? The answer is short and sweet— *laziness.* Lack of consideration comes into play, but "F"s are lazy and that's why they litter. You will *not* find a conscientious, thoughtful person who litters . . . period.

Smokers flicking cigarette butts are a classic example. I'll grant you cigarettes are biodegradable and it's rare that fires are set off by this impertinence, but it's rooted in laziness . . . no ifs, ands, or butts.

⊕ The Coke® Was on Me

Speaking of litter, I was driving down a four-lane divided highway, making a pass on the right because, as usual, an "F" was hogging the left lane. I had almost reached a minivan's rear bumper when I saw its passenger window roll down. Out came a hand holding a fast-food soda cup, which was then turned over to empty its contents.

Since we were traveling at approximately 55 mph, the soda flew back and covered the front of my car, including the windshield. Clearly the Coke® was on me.

I pulled up alongside the "F"s, beeping to get their attention. It took multiple tries for my horn to be heard above their blaring radio. When they finally noticed me, they appeared utterly clueless as to why on *earth* I would be honking at them. I received blank, "what are you looking at" stares in response to my "what-an-F" hand gesture.

They, themselves, were nothing but trash . . .

Little Big Man

Here's more evidence that large vehicles are often occupied by small minds.

One morning last year I pulled into my office building parking lot. As usual, my commute had been hampered by a slew of "F"s, so by the time I arrived I was in no mood to waste any *more* time.

I drove past the building and zipped into my usual parking spot. Just as I did, a yellow Humvee (no lie—school-bus yellow) appeared from the other side of the building. He was barely moving, I might add.

Sure, I could have stopped to let him go first, but that would have wasted my time and saved him none.

To be clear, let me reiterate that he was *crawling* and we probably never came any closer to each other than about 25 feet.

I parked, got out of my car, and started walking toward my building.

And there, blocking my path, sat the Humvee with its passenger-side window rolled down.

Me entering parking lot

Hummer crawling around corner of building

My path blocked... window rolled down

The conversation with Little Big Man:

LBM: "You almost got that little Jeep of yours crushed just now."

Me: "Do we know each other?"

LBM: (puzzled look) "No?"

Me: "Then try to imagine how much I care what you think."

LBM: "Maybe next time you'll cause an accident!"

Me: "Do you *think* I didn't notice the bright yellow Hummer?"

LBM: Silence.

Me: "You were driving slowly, I was driving quickly, so apparently I value my time more than you do."

LBM: "You're acting like an jerk."

Me: "No . . . I'm acting like someone who's going to stop talking to you now."

I pulled a pad and pen from my briefcase, walked to the front of his vehicle, and made it clear that I was writing down his license plate number. I waved my hand in disgust and said, "Move along before I call the cops." I thought I heard a fly buzzing around my head as I walked away, but then I realized that the "F" was still yapping. Luckily the **"F"-INATOR** was nearby . . .

They've Got Us over a Barrel

Another notorious group are those "F"s who grossly overcharge for basic commodities. For example, the entire planet continues to experience a major monetary shift due to these selfish, small-minded, and nonproductive "F"s. I'm endlessly amazed by the incredible talent it must take for "F"s to hold the world hostage with oil to which they've injected essentially *zero added value*. It's frankly pathetic.

Because of this, expert analysts indicate that smaller cars have now become a core segment of the automobile industry, which represents the most dramatic shift in consumer demand in decades. As we struggle with the concept of paying more to feed our vehicles than to feed our families, many of us will choose to downsize in order to save money and reduce emissions. The roads, therefore, will become even more dangerous as we cross paths with those who continue to drive behemoths.

We all need to do our part in keeping each other safe and keeping road rage emotions at bay.

> ❯ "F"s, your driving blunders can now wreak more havoc than before, so it's time for you to step it up! Focus on the road, pay more attention, and control your aggression.

> ❯ "A"s, although smaller vehicles tend to be more nimble in accident avoidance, remember that with downsizing comes less protection. Now more than ever, we must take advantage of our inn-"A"-te skills to stay out of harm's way. Anticipate that "F"s will continue to drive like idiots—presume that if there's a wrong move to make, they'll make it.

Whatever we drive, those of us in Class A possess a keen driving aptitude that "F"s do not. We *will* prevail!

EXIT 15

Let's Make a Deal

Although this final EXIT does not directly relate to "over-the-road" struggles, I've included it here since purchasing a vehicle can sometimes be even more frustrating than operating one.

Vehicle salespeople often have terrible reputations that are largely undeserved. Most of them are regular folks like you and me, just trying to earn an honest living. But the following "F"-isodes, all of them true accounts of test drives with a friend, unfortunately do nothing but reinforce the used-car salesman stereotype.

Yakety Yak (Don't Talk Back)

Some vehicle salespeople drive me crazy because they *never . . . shut . . . up.* They are "F"s who believe that talking should precede listening. They answer questions that I haven't asked, yet they don't answer the ones I *do* ask. Not only are they oblivious to competing models' specifications, they rarely understand even their own. (*"An MP3 port, you say? Not sure I'm familiar with that there technology."*)

Their incessant yakking prevents me from judging the vehicle's interior sound level . . . I can't evaluate the sound system . . . I can barely hear myself think!

One of their more puzzling tactics is this: they attempt to sell me a vehicle *before* I've driven it. Imagine a conversation with one of them as a realtor:

Him: "Well, Dave, would you like to buy that house?"

Me: "Um, you haven't taken me to see it yet."

Him: "Oh, let's not get bogged down with details. I just know you'll love it!"

"F"s, here's the deal: If I don't like the way a vehicle feels, handles, sounds, and performs, then *no* amount of information you share is valuable. Every . . . single . . . thing you say is useless noise until *after* I've driven the vehicle and decided it's a candidate.

The way the process *should* work:

(a) We exchange greetings.

(b) You say, "Which model would you like to drive?" (And you should at *all* times, for *every* model you sell, have several test cars prepped, fueled, and ready to go so I don't have to wait for you to locate one on the lot.)

(c) We drive it.

(d) You ask, "Now that you've driven the car, is this a model you'd consider owning?"

(e) If I answer yes, you ask, "Is there anything I can tell you about the car that you don't already know?" (This is *critical* . . . when you ramble on with information that I already have, you're only wasting more of my time.)

(f) If I answer no, you say, "Have a nice day" and you *leave me alone.*

Got it, Yak?

I'd Like You to Meet My Manager

This next ploy must work on the general "F" population since almost *every* vehicle dealership now follows this practice. Somehow it's no longer sufficient for the car-buying public to deal with a lone salesperson. No, you're now urged to "meet their manager" before you leave the lot.

How excited "F"s must become as they think, "Ooh . . . I get to meet the manager? Clearly I'm very special!" This routine must lead to sales as a manager swoops in and offers a "Special deal . . . today only . . . because you seem like such nice, deserving people."

For those of us in Class A, this is another serious waste of time. F-ailspeople attempt to put this under the guise of "having someone else here at the dealership who will give you personal care if I'm not available," but a line like that has the opposite effect on those of us with intelligence and judgment.

"F"s, remember this: we in Class A actually value our time, so when you corral us into staying longer than *we* want to, you drastically reduce the chances that we'll ever set foot in your dealership again.

Salespeople should be trained to distinguish between Class-A and Class-F customers. I guarantee you it would increase business. If we were treated properly the first time, we might actually come *back*.

You know, to meet your manager.

Mm hmm.

The Lessor of Two (or Three) Evils

For the well-educated, leasing can be a viable alternative to buying a new vehicle. But for those in our society who don't happen to be proficient with numbers or who lack their fair share of common sense, leasing can be yet another dealer scam.

Evil #1

Telling people that leases don't carry an interest rate. What do car dealers call it? Oh yes, a "money factor." Here's a tip: this factor was invented by dealers who wanted to hide a lease's true interest rate and thereby scam the public. A lease's interest rate can be determined by multiplying this money factor by 2,400. It's that simple—so don't let them tell you otherwise.

Evil #2

Lowering a lease's monthly payment by inflating the required down payment. There ought to be a law requiring that all leases be advertised as requiring zero money down. The general buying public can't accurately compare leases with differing down payments. Even when using a computer it takes a reasonable degree of knowledge. Here's a quick example:

Lease term:	**3 years**	
Interest rate:	**7%**	Monthly Payment with **$0** down: **~$400**
Sell price:	**$25,000**	Monthly Payment with **$2,500** (10%) down: **~$320**
Residual:	**$15,000**	

The uneducated might see this and say, "Wow, if I put 10 percent down, I can lower my payment by 20 percent!" Don't fall for it. The math only works this way because of the residual. *Any* time you compare leases, require each dealer to quote you a monthly payment with no money down. (And don't forget to compare fees.)

Evil #3

Forcing consumers to absorb the full cost of dealer options into the lease period. This is another scam. These options tend to be completely unnecessary items like door-edge protection, for example. Let's think this through . . . the dealer feels no shame in persuading you to buy the option even though its value will be virtually nothing by the end of a three-year lease? Uh huh. By making you fully absorb such an option within the lease period, *only* the dealer wins . . . they receive a vehicle off lease with (in this case) better door edges, meaning they can resell it for more money. There is no benefit to you whatsoever.

Let me ask you this: do you know any poor car dealers? No, neither do I. These evils are a few of the reasons why not.

Yeah, Your Golf Clubs Will Fit

My friend Mike and I visited a Mazda dealership to check out a Miata. I was looking for a small car capable of carrying at least one set of golf clubs but preferably two. We were trying to hold a private conversation when our space was rudely invaded by the nearest salesman. And so it went:

Salesman: "What do you think?"

Me: "About what?"

Salesman: "The Miata. Do you like it?"

Me: "I don't know yet. We just got here."

Mike: "I don't think your clubs will fit."

Me: "No, you're right, they won't."

Salesman: "They'll fit!"

Me: (startled by his interruption) "What?"

Salesman: "Your clubs will fit."

Me: "No, they clearly won't. I can see that the trunk's too small for my bag."

Salesman: (yelling across the showroom) "Hey, Joe, will his clubs fit into a Miata?"

Joe: (yelling back) "Yeah, they'll fit."

Salesman: (turning back to me) "See? I *told* you they'd fit."

As we held in our laughter, Mike and I convulsed as if preventing ourselves from sneezing aloud. We immediately exited the dealership with the "F" tailing us all the way out to the parking lot, imploring us to reconsider.

As we drove away, Mike and I confirmed to each other that we, in fact, *had* reconsidered . . . we still thought the guy was an idiot.

You See . . . This Window's Open but That One's Closed

In this "F"-isode, Mike and I went to a Subaru dealership back when the SVX was first introduced. If you remember, this car's gimmick was that it featured a "window within a window" in each door.

Like the first ant to locate food at a picnic, a salesman sprinted over as soon as we arrived and another conversation began:

Him: "Ain't she a beauty?"

Us: Silence.

Him: "Have you seen the new SVX?"

Us: "Yes."

Him: "What can I tell you about it?"

Us: "Nothing. We've read all about it in the car mags . . . we just stopped in to see one in person."

Him: (ignoring our answer to his prior question) "It has a window within a window!"

Us: "We know . . . we've read about that."

Him: (first poking his hand inside the car through the smaller open window) "You see . . . this window's open . . ." (then poking his finger *into* the glass of the closed upper window) ". . . but that one's closed."

Thank goodness he was there to point out the difference between transparent glass and air! Mike and I turned away in disgust and left without uttering another word.

What Would You Say If I Could Give You That Car at Half Price?

Last one . . . Toyota this time. As Mike and I entered the dealership, we were greeted by an attractive, petite brunette holding a cup of coffee. She offered to help us, and we responded by asking to speak with a salesman. She enthusiastically replied, "I'm a salesperson!" We were thrilled.

The upside? We were test driving a Supra that day and she was able to fit in the back seat. Unfortunately, though, she never stopped talking. I can no longer remember all of the mindless ramblings she threw our way during that test drive, but at one point she felt it necessary to point out the radio buttons to us. (*"Thanks, we hadn't noticed those. Do they cost extra?"*)

Back at the dealership, she practically begged us to sit down with her to "share our feelings":

Her: "Did you like the car?"

Us: "Yes."

Her: "Are there any features I can explain to you?"

Us: "No." (Mike and I read auto publications every week and every month, so we always know what we're getting ourselves into . . . literally. In fact, that should be question #1 from every car dealer to save boatloads of time: "Do you read car magazines?")

Her: "Well, then, just one more question . . . what would you say if I could give you that car at half price?"

Me: "I'll take it . . . and I'll pay cash."

Her: (hesitating) "No, no . . . I meant . . . I'm talking about cutting your payment in half."

Mike: "Um . . . might you be talking about leasing, by any chance?" (Leasing was not nearly as prevalent back then as it is now.)

Her: (bubble burst) "Why, yes!"

This time Mike and I couldn't keep from laughing before we'd even gotten up from the table.

When will dealers learn that it's good business to separate the wheat from the chaff, to differentiate between "A"s and "F"s? That experience cost them a Supra sale . . . I drove straight back to a Porsche dealership and bought a 968 instead, primarily because of the way I'd been treated.

GLOSSARY

Every important social movement tends to bring with it an entirely new vernacular. The Why It's Your Fault™ crusade is no exception. What follows is a compilation of key terms and phrases used throughout this book. I recommend that you refer to this glossary on a regular basis.

"A"-daptive cruise control—revolutionary technology that would allow a trailing vehicle (driven by a member Class A) to "push" a leading vehicle (driven by an "F") when it was traveling too slowly, thereby improving everyone's safety and enjoyment.

Alice in Dunderland—a man named Alice who impotently decelerates whenever he sees a police cruiser approaching him from behind on a highway.

backseat driver—a passenger who feels compelled to offer suggestions and criticisms to a driver. Backseat drivers only have merit when an "F" is behind the wheel.

blind leading the blind—an unobservant "F" who carelessly steers into an adjacent lane, unaware that a second clueless "F" is already in that lane hovering in his blind spot.

Boolean logic—simplistically, the language of "if-thens," "ands," "ors," and "buts." Boolean logic is the basis of algebra, computer science, law, and philosophy. An example from this book is "All dogs are mammals, but not all mammals are dogs." Every dog is a mammal, but some mammals (like humans) are clearly not dogs. To find a misapplication of Boolean logic, take EXIT 12.

bored walk—"F"s inconsiderately walking down the middle of a parking lot aisle, especially when they're fully aware that vehicles are trying to proceed past them.

bull** by the horn**—a label for "F"s who overuse their vehicle horns after failing to anticipate problematic situations.

burn rubber—what this author feels should be the fate of all rubberneckers.

cars only—a toll booth lane that only cars are permitted to use. "F"s commonly misinterpret this as a lane that cars are *required* to use, which fortunately leaves other lanes less congested for those of us in Class A.

cart behind the horse's ass—a shopping cart abandoned in a parking space vacated by an "F".

centrifugal force—a force that acts on any mass accelerating around a rotational reference frame, as with vehicles driving around curved exit ramps. This force has a dark side that occurs when "F"s drive far too slowly around such ramps.

chain of fools—a line of "F"s that forms in the right lane at a red light while the left lane remains empty.

char-"F"-teristics—traits of all "F"s, which by default are inherently negative.

chip off the old blockhead—an "F" who, as taught by his inconsiderate parents, blocks one traffic lane while waiting for the other direction to clear.

Class A—people who care enough about others and the world around them to *feel* frustration.

Class F—the inconsiderate and annoying people who *cause* frustration and road rage. Class F consists of morons, twits, and jerks (see EXIT 1).

cloverleaf—a grouping of circular exit/entrance ramps connecting perpendicular roadways, which from overhead simulates the shape of a four-leaf clover.

cold cuts—any situation whereby a cold "F" intentionally cuts off another driver.

considerate idiot—an excessively considerate "F" who forces multiple vehicles behind him to wait while he waves a single driver ahead.

cosmetic improvements—superficial measures taken by "F"s to improve their outward appearance. Unfortunately, "F"s tend to make these improvements (e.g., putting on makeup, shaving, combing their hair) while driving.

Darwinism—see "natural selection."

delay of game—a penalty that should be assessed when an "F" tailgates another vehicle over an extended distance even though parallel highway lanes are completely devoid of traffic.

Doppler effect—the reduction in perceived pitch as a sound source moves away from you. Well-known examples are a train whistle and an emergency vehicle siren, which seemingly drop in pitch as they move into the distance. Only an "F" will lay on his vehicle horn long enough to create the Doppler effect. (See "bull**** by the horn.")

dummy—the role in a game of bridge for which "F"s are perfectly suited (pun intended).

exit strategy—in warfare, a plan to remove troops from battle; in business, a scheme to terminate ownership in a company; on the road, the process of anticipating a highway exit.

"F" Meter—a Why It's Your Fault™ device that categorizes and measures the severity of "F" behavior.

"F" Troop—a classic television show from the mid-1960s; in this book, it denotes a collection of nitwits who ineffectually imitate the functions of legitimate police officers. The most notable example is traffic cops for hire.

"F"-INATOR—a gigantic, imaginary vehicle equipped with an arsenal of power tools that it uses to punish "F"s in a manner that those of us in Class A can only dream about. The **"F"-INATOR** is the world's first Fault Utility Vehicle, or "FUV."

"F"-isode—an episode involving an "F".

fast food—food that should not be served to slow people.

frustrated—a condition in which members of Class A regularly find themselves, solely attributable to the repetitive, irritating actions of "F"s.

FUV—an acronym for Fault Utility Vehicle.

◄Grateful Dead►—a bumper sticker reminding drivers to always pass eighteen-wheelers on the left; an American rock band from the San Francisco Bay Area.

gray matter—another term for brain tissue. It's a scientific fact that only "F"s have gray matter, befitting their fuzzy, vague perspective on the world. Crystal-clear thinking on the part of Class-A drivers stems from the fact that their brain matter is actually black and white, just like their reasoning.

grid-irony—foolish "F" tailgating maneuvers.

HOV—an acronym for High Occupancy Vehicle. Running adjacent to regular highway traffic lanes, HOV lanes are reserved for vehicles with more than one occupant. They are sometimes referred to as "commuter" lanes. Whatever the label, they're lanes from which "F"s should be permanently banned.

hurry up and wait—a condition whereby an "F" pulls out in front of another driver only to then drive below the posted speed limit.

I don't care what you think—a phrase that every Class A member should use if ever confronted by an "F" (trust me … it drives them crazy).

idiom—a ridiculous, obsolete phrase such as "haste makes waste."

idiot—a person who believes in ridiculous, obsolete phrases.

***Idiot*arod**—in contrast to the Iditarod (the world's foremost dogsled race), the *Idiot*arod designates any instance of "F"s failing to drive safely and effectively in the snow.

in a hurry—a state in which "A"s commonly exist, due primarily to their admirable desire to achieve. "F"s often mistake speed for aggression, which feeds the common misconception that fast drivers are the culprits behind road rage.

inn-"A"-teness—a natural driving intelligence present in all "A"s from birth.

incomplete p(ass)—a situation created when a Class-A player pulls over to let a tailgating "F" go by, but the "F" fails to complete the pass. This leads to traffic congestion as passing lanes are blocked.

in-"F"-titude—absurdity, foolishness, and general incompetence—traits that are common (and amplified) in "F"s.

instinct—an inborn pattern of behavior common to a given biological species. Since "F"s possess horrible instincts, scientists theorize that they must have evolved from a more limited gene pool than those of us in Class A.

It takes a village—the first half of a proverb that ends "to raise a child," implying that society is partially responsible for raising children and not the family alone; also, the first half of an Allan proverb that ends "to raise a village idiot," which states, not merely implies, that the global population of "F"s is solely responsible for raising more of their own kind.

Jersey barriers—three-foot-tall poured concrete barriers used to separate traffic lanes; originally developed in Hoboken, N.J.

Keystone Cops—poorly trained "cops for hire" who bumble their way through whatever task they've been assigned (also see "F" Troop).

Lazy—the little-known eighth dwarf; also, an adjective commonly applied to "F"s.

le-"F"-t turn—a left turn *not* made (even though there is sufficient time to do so) because an "F" chooses to wait for oncoming vehicles to take a right turn first.

linear thinking—the inability of "F"s to multiprocess (i.e., consider more than one variable at a time), thereby reducing their ability to anticipate and avoid problematic situations.

little big man—a person who drives a large vehicle to compensate for mental or physical shortcomings.

money factor—when multiplied by 2,400 this will yield an auto lease's interest rate.

moron roller coaster—when an "F" emulates cruise control by keeping his accelerator pedal in exactly the same position, which results in his speed fluctuating wildly over inclines and declines in a roadway.

natural selection—the force behind evolution that preserves the best traits—and weeds out the worst—of a particular species through successive generations. If a car thief (a.k.a. an "F") were to drive into a telephone pole during a police chase, that would be an example of natural selection successfully weeding out a defective member from the human species. (Also known as "Darwinism.")

need to impede—an inherent trait in "F"s that compels them to waste other peoples' time without good reason.

nervous breakdown—"F"s who speed along breakdown lanes during traffic jams as others wait patiently; "F"s who immediately commence changing a flat tire no matter where it occurs, even if it places them directly in harm's way.

never-ending story—turn signals that continue blinking long after an "F" has made a turn or changed lanes; windshield wipers that are left running after it has stopped raining.

O.K. TO PASS—a new sign that should be installed on every school bus, to be used by its driver whenever traffic backs up behind the bus. Once kids have safely made their way clear of the current stop, this sign would indicate that it is safe to pass the bus before it proceeds to its next stop.

Objects in Mirror Are More Pissed Off Than They Appear—a message that should be stamped onto the mirrors of every vehicle owned by an "F".

obtuse—an adjective used to describe certain angles (between 90 and 180 degrees) and all "F"s (slow to learn or understand).

oxymoron—a combination of incongruous or contradictory terms. "Common courtesy" has become an oxymoron since courtesy in "F"s is uncommon.

pain in the gas—any gas station pain caused by "F"s and experienced by "A"s. Examples include attendants who carelessly drip gas onto vehicles, people who stop at the first open pump instead of politely driving forward, and twits who leave their vehicles at the pump while they go "shopping."

p(ass) interference—any situation whereby an "F" intentionally prevents someone from passing them on a highway.

pass/fail grading—a simplistic grading system adopted (by "F"s) when normal grading is thought to promote "undesirable competition for grades of high quality, which could cause less learning for some students." Put another way, it is a grading system inherently designed to discourage excellence. Pass/fail grading has proven to be successful only when applied to the human race, as was done in this book (and in the complete Why It's Your Fault™ series).

Pavlov—a Russian scientist who first discovered the phenomenon known as "conditional reflexes." His work involved the measurement of salivation in dogs as they responded to external stimuli (a ringing bell, which had previously signaled the arrival of food). "F"s display erroneous conditioned responses to basic stimuli on the road.

perfect storm—a tempest caused when two "F"s reach a common juncture, neither having had the foresight to anticipate a coordinated merge.

PITA—an acronym for Pain In The Ass.

Preparation "F"—the proposed brand name to be used if a product is ever proven effective in curing road rage.

Queen of Hearts—the fictional foul-tempered monarch from *Alice in Wonderland* who would scream, "Off with their heads!" as she decreed death sentences to her inferior subjects (who, by the way, I'm sure were "F"s).

right-of-way—a concept whereby one driver has the right to use a section of road to the exclusion of another. This does *not* mean that people on the right-hand side always go first … "right" in this case indicates propriety, not direction.

road rage—an emotion of intense frustration attributable solely to the repetitive, inane actions of "F"s. Road rage in members of Class A refers to the emotion only. Violent or aggressive behavior is only displayed by weak-minded "F"s when they fail to *control* their emotions.

road warriors—this group includes firefighters, police officers, EMTs, parcel and mail delivery personnel, truckers, tradesmen, bus and limousine drivers, and tow truck and snowplow operators . . . essentially anyone whose very job involves driving.

roadpourri—a collection of miscellaneous road rage "F"-isodes.

rotary—a one-way circular "roundabout" intersecting a series of roadways and intended to facilitate a continual flow of traffic. Common sense and law indicates that entering traffic must yield to vehicles already within a rotary. When encountered by "F"s, however, a rotary becomes the ultimate, definitive, unequivocal, and irrefutable worst case bungling of simultaneous merging and yielding.

roughing the passer—an action that should be taken against "F"s when they make an incomplete pass.

rubberneck(er)—an "F" who can't bear to drive past an accident scene without slowing down to gawk.

Scarlet Letter—the nineteenth-century novel by Nathaniel Hawthorne in which an adulterous woman was forced to wear the letter "A" as a badge of shame. Had Hawthorne been a man before his time, the scarlet letter would have been an "F", as it is in this book.

Slow and Steady Wins the Race—one of Aesop's (fallacious) fables. As it turns out, Aesop was sometimes a bit confused, as evidenced by the fact that a tortoise never beats a hare in reality.

slow people—those who should not be served fast food.

small mind—that which is possessed by "F"s who use large vehicles to intimidate other drivers.

Snagglepuss—a pink, anthropomorphic mountain lion from the old Hanna-Barbera cartoon series. It was known for the catchphrase, "Exit . . . stage left (or right)." Little did it know that these "exit" catchphrases would one day relate to road rage.

speed demon—an "F" who intentionally accelerates to prevent someone from passing him on a two-lane road.

speed trap—a police strategy used to entrap people (including citizens of Class A) into involuntarily contributing to a government's revenue pool. Wild, aggressive drivers should be ticketed . . . people who drive too slowly should be ticketed . . . but people who cautiously and safely exceed posted speeds should be spared. Officers and courts should be trained to separate "A"s from "F"s and should treat them accordingly.

Speedy Guns Alice—a wimp who demonstrates a hyper-aversion to speed guns, instinctively hitting his brakes even when a speed trap is located on the *opposite* side of a highway.

steering from the rudder—management terminology used to describe executives who run their companies from "behind the scenes"; also, the process of easing congestion by consciously adjusting your speed in the right lane, thereby preventing an "F" from matching your speed in the left lane.

steering wheel—the device that should be your first tool in avoiding an accident, as it is far more effective than brakes in most situations.

transponder—a device carried in or affixed to a vehicle that is automatically recognized by "EZ Pass" or "Fast Lane" toll booth systems.

truck me all to hell—a phrase commonly uttered in response to offensive conduct on the part of rogue "F" truckers.

tunnel vision—self-afflicted, sudden blindness in "F"s who fail to remove their sunglasses when driving into a dark tunnel.

turn signal—a device that indicates to other drivers what the heck you intend to do next. "F"s seem oblivious to the fact that vehicles come equipped with turn signals.

Twits Family Robinson—any family in which parents fail to teach their children how to be considerate.

two by two—a new and improved road rule for handling four-way stops. Vehicles should proceed two at a time through such an intersection, which would cut everyone's wait time nearly in half.

uneasy riders—Class-A bikers whose safety is jeopardized by the bonehead maneuvers of "F"s.

unsportsmanlike conduct—a penalty that should be assessed when an "F" immediately pulls into the lane of a vehicle he has just passed, which causes that vehicle's driver to involuntarily tailgate.

wrong turn on red—a right turn on red taken by an "F" even when vehicles are coming from the other direction; also, a situation in which the left lane at a red light is empty but an "F" who intends to go straight waits in the right lane instead, thereby preventing others from taking a right turn.

yakety yak—the incessant chatter of uninformed, inconsiderate car salespeople.

Yield—a triangular-shaped sign which indicates that other drivers should be allowed to proceed first. Some "F"s routinely confuse this with the more common eight-sided stop sign; other "F"s ignore yield signs completely.

LAST RIGHTS

f you enjoyed this book, or at the very least could relate to it, congratulations. You may consider yourself a proud member of Class A!

If you didn't, then you're an "F" and the rest of us don't care *what* you think.

And now that my book is done, it's time for me to focus my time and energy on a new venture . . . coming up with a cure for these highway hemorrhoids.

I know just what I'll call it:

Preparation "F"

What else does the future hold for me? Rest assured . . . I'll continue documenting the harebrained habits of "F"'s for as long as I'm able . . .

. . . or maybe even longer.